Cheater's Guide to
Speaking
English
Like a Native

Other Books by Boyé Lafayette De Mente

Cheater's Guide to
Speaking
English
Like a Native

Boyé Lafayette De Mente

TUTTLE PUBLISHING
Tokyo • Rutland, Vermont • Singapore

Published by Tuttle Publishing, an imprint of Periplus Editions (HK) Ltd., with editorial offices at 364 Innovation Drive, North Clarendon, Vermont 05759 and 130 Joo Seng Road, #06-01, Singapore 368357.

ISBN-10: 0-8048-3682-5
ISBN-13: 978-0-8048-3682-1

Distributed by

North America, Latin America & Europe
Tuttle Publishing
364 Innovation Drive
North Clarendon, VT 05759-9436, USA
Tel: 1 (802) 773-8930   Fax: 1 (802) 773-6993
info@tuttlepublishing.com
www.tuttlepublishing.com

Japan
Tuttle Publishing
Yaekari Building, 3rd Floor
5-4-12 Osaki, Shinagawa-ku, Tokyo 141 0032
Tel: (81) 03 5437-0171   Fax: (81) 03 5437-0755
tuttle-sales@gol.com

Asia Pacific
Berkeley Books Pte. Ltd.
130 Joo Seng Road, #06-01, Singapore 368357
Tel: (65) 6280-1330   Fax: (65) 6280-6290
inquiries@periplus.com.sg
www.periplus.com

Printed in Singapore
10 09 08 07   6 5 4 3 2 1

TUTTLE PUBLISHING® is a registered trademark of Tuttle Publishing, a division of Periplus Editions (HK) Ltd.

Contents

8

14

A bird in the hand

This is an old saying that comes from the sport of bird hunting. When one bird is shot, the others fly away. It is another way of saying that it is better to achieve one goal than try to do too much and gain nothing.

a. *A bird in the hand is worth two in the bush.*
b. *Let's go for a bird in the hand and forget the rest.*
c. *He was never satisfied with a bird in the hand, and went on to become very successful.*

A little bird told me

This is a phrase used to conceal the identity of someone who has told you something that was previously confidential or secret.

a. *A little bird told me, and you might as well stop asking because I'm not going to tell you who the little bird was!*
b. *I heard it from a little bird.*
c. *Your little bird is nothing but a tattle tale.*

A miss is as good as a mile

This expression originally referred to being shot at and the bullet just barely missing you. It is now used in reference to a variety of negative things that could have happened but didn't.

a. *When I left just before the earthquake I really appreciated that a miss is as good as a mile.*
b. *When his wife showed up just seconds after his girlfriend left he smiled and said to himself that a miss is as good as a mile!*
c. *When a speeding car almost hits you, a miss is not as good as a mile!*

A needle in a haystack

Something or somebody that is difficult to find.

a. *Trying to find him in that crowd would be like searching for a needle in a haystack!*
b. *Finding something in this store is like looking for a needle in a haystack.*
c. *Finding your office was like looking for a needle in a haystack.*

A nightcap

A nightcap is a euphemism for an alcoholic drink taken just before the evening ends. It is often used in movies when a man or woman invites someone to come into their home or apartment after an evening out on the town, giving it strong sexual overtones. In essence, it means to "cap off" an evening with a final drink.

a. *It's still early! How about a nightcap?*
b. *You're interested in more than just a nightcap, aren't you!*
c. *Your problem is that you have one nightcap after another!*

Ace in the hole

An advantage in a game or business that is kept in reserve, or secret until it is needed to ensure victory. The saying comes from the card game of poker.

a. *That guy always has an ace in the hole!*
b. *He always comes up with an ace in the hole.*
c. *What I need now is an ace in the hole.*

Across the board

This expression derives from a reference to the entire width of a board, and may mean everything and everybody.

a. *The pay raise was across the board. Everybody got a hike in pay.*
b. *He made an across-the-board accusation, blaming everybody on the team.*
c. *His criticism was across the board. He left nobody out.*

Act like a spring chicken

Acting young, energetic; often said of older men and women who begin acting like they are young again.

a. *Stop trying to act like a spring chicken! You're making a fool of yourself!*
b *You're a grandmother acting like a spring chicken!*
c. *That old man is still acting like a spring chicken.*

Acting fishy

Fish, especially small fish, habitually dart here and there, making it difficult to predict which way they are going to go next. This led to "acting fishy" being applied to people who behave in a suspicious manner.

a. *The guy in front of the bank was acting fishy, so someone called the police.*
b. *She said she didn't like you because you looked fishy.*
c. *My wife can spot fishy behavior a mile away!*

Actions speak louder than words

Generally, what you do is far more important, and far more influential, than what you say.

a. *Never mind what he says. Wait until you see what he does. Actions speaker louder than words.*
b. *Who ever said actions speak louder than words must have been thinking about you!*
c. *When it comes to politics, actions definitely speak louder than words!*

After one's own heart

This expression is used to describe someone with whom you agree on many or most things. You might say your hearts beat in harmony.

a. *My new boss loves to go fishing every weekend. He is a man after my own heart.*
b. *I was very pleased to find out that the boss was a man after my own heart.*
c. *It is always a special pleasure to spend time with friends who are after your own heart.*

Airing dirty laundry

When couples and others become estranged and begin revealing unsavory and damaging facts about each other it is commonly said that they are airing their dirty laundry.

a. *Let's not air our dirty laundry!*
b. *After that couple broke up they aired all of their dirty laundry.*
c. *All she does is air her dirty laundry!*

All rolled into one

"All rolled into one" refers to multiple duties, obligations or efforts being pursued at the same time, often by just one person.

a. *His brother is president and vice-president all rolled into one.*
b. *When I realized that I had been given several jobs all rolled into one I didn't know whether to say thanks or no thank you.*
c. *Here are our problems, all rolled into one.*

All shook up

This expression refers to being emotionally upset, usually in a negative sense.

a. *She got all shook up when she heard the news.*
b. *Don't get all shook up about it!*
c. *You look all shook up. What happened?*

All wrapped up in himself

People who are "all wrapped up" in themselves are egocentric and do not think about the feelings or needs of others.

a. *You shouldn't date that guy! He's too wrapped up in himself!*
b. *He's so wrapped up in himself nobody likes him.*
c. *She can't stand men who are wrapped up in themselves.*

An accident waiting to happen

Someone or something that can go seriously wrong without warning, often said of a person who is accident prone, or who is under serious emotional pressure that might cause him or her to do something violent.

a. *That new off-road vehicle is an accident waiting to happen!*
b. *He's an accident waiting to happen.*
c. *I knew he was an accident waiting to happen when I first met him.*

An also-ran

Very common in the political area, an also-ran refers to someone who runs for a political office and fails, or someone in office who fails to get re-elected.

a. *Forget him! He's going to be an also-ran!*
b. *After becoming an also-ran it's hard to make a comeback.*
c. *It's interesting that political also-rans often become university professors.*

Another day another dollar

During the American depression of the 1930s people were lucky to have a job. Many found work only occasionally and were paid one dollar a day, giving birth to the comment. Now, the saying refers to the relief felt after finishing another day of hard work.

a. *I had to work overtime and all I can say is another day another dollar!*
b. *It was a really rough day but another day another dollar.*
c. *I'm just trying to hang in because another day is another dollar.*

Ante up

This term comes from the game of poker, and refers to the amount of money you must put into the pool before receiving cards or additional cards. It also refers to paying one's share, and includes the sense of paying up front, in advance.

a. *If you want to stay in the game you have to ante up.*
b. *He had to ante up to buy into that deal.*
c. *If you can't ante up you're out of the game.*

Ants in the pants

People who get ants in their pants are very likely to go through a series of quick and convulsive actions to get rid of them.

a. *You're running around like you have ants in your pants!*
b. *Can't you be still? You act like you have ants in your pants!*
c. *Some kids seem to be born with ants in their pants!*

Apple of one's eye

When buying apples it is common to select those that are the most attractive in size, color and overall appearance. This led to the expression "the apple of one's eye" in reference to something or someone that one is especially fond of.

a. *His youngest daughter was the apple of his eye.*
b. *Because she was the apple of his eye her brothers and sisters were jealous.*
c. *It was pretty obvious that the new secretary was the apple of the boss's eye.*

As American as apple pie

Apple pie has traditionally been regarded as the quintessential American dessert because apples were common, it was easy to prepare in wood-burning stoves, and it was usually delicious. Thus, anything that was typically American came to be compared to apple pie.

a. *A famous black writer once said that violence was as American as apple pie!*
b. *Baseball is as American as apple pie.*
c. *Many immigrants become as American as apple pie in two or three years.*

As clean as a whistle

This expression refers to something that disappears or is "cleaned up" without leaving a trace, as the sound of a whistle leaves nothing behind.

a. *The bank robber got away as clean as a whistle.*
b. *She left his wallet as clean as a whistle.*
c. *The house was as clean as a whistle.*

As crooked as a dog's hind leg

The back legs of dogs are crooked, thus the saying, which refers to someone who engages in illegal behavior.

a. *That guy is as crooked as a dog's hind leg!*
b. *Politicians often appear to be as crooked as a dog's hind leg.*
c. *He gave the impression of being as crooked as a dog's hind leg.*

As cute as a bug's ear

I have no idea if any bug has cute ears, but it is common to describe an unusually pretty infant or a small baby as "cute as a bug's ear."

a. *The baby took after its mother, and was as cute as a bug's ear.*
b. *He likes girls who are as cute as a bug's ear.*
c. *That advertisement is as cute as a bug's ear.*

As dead as a door nail

Something or somebody who is not moving, motionless, doesn't expend any energy; is dead.

a. *As soon as he opened his mouth I knew my idea was as dead as a door nail.*
b. *My relationship with her is as dead as a door nail.*
c. *What's wrong? You act like you're as dead as a door nail.*

As easy as falling off a log

Something that is very easy to do; from the fact that it is very difficult to stand on a log that is floating in water—an old way of transporting logs.

a. *Don't worry about it! It's as easy as falling off a log!*
b. *Anybody can do it! It's as easy as falling off a log.*
c. *You said skiing was as easy as falling off a log but I broke my leg!*

As flat as a pancake

This may be said of a tire, a balloon and a number of other things, including a woman's breasts. In the latter instance, it is not complimentary and may be considered in a very negative light.

a. *Our sales results last year were as flat as a pancake.*
b. *You hurt that girl when you said she was as flat-chested as a pancake.*
c. *My left rear tire was as flat as a pancake.*

As good as gold

When something is exceptionally valuable it is common to say it is as good as gold.

a. *When I bought the stock I was told it was as good as gold.*
b. *If you want an investment that is as good as gold buy a house.*
c. *His word is as good as gold.*

As guilty as sin

In Christian theology, one may be guilty of many different kinds of transgressions, but not all "bad acts" are regarded as "sins"—that is, acts that are directly against the "laws of God." When someone is described as being "as guilty as sin," the condemnation is very strong.

a. *The charges were dismissed, but everybody knew he was as guilty as sin.*
b. *I can tell from the look on your face that you're as guilty as sin!*
c. *You say you are innocent but I know you are as guilty as sin.*

As pretty as a picture

Saying that someone or something is as pretty as a picture is a high compliment.

a. *My girlfriend is as pretty as a picture.*
b. *You told me she was as pretty as a picture!*
c. *The whole scene, the park and children playing, was as pretty as a picture.*

As slick as a greased pig

In some rural areas of the United States there used to be a sporting event in which pigs in large pens were smeared with grease and turned loose. Boys and men would try to catch and hold them. This gave rise to a saying that someone who was hard to catch and hold was as slick as a greased pig.

a. *She's never going to pin that guy down! He's as slick as a greased pig!*
b. *Politicians make a profession of being as slick as greased pigs.*
c. *Trying to get a decision out of that guy is like trying to catch a greased pig!*

As slow as molasses

When molasses gets cold it becomes thick and stiff, and pours very slowly; now used to describe people and things that move slowly.

a. *My first Internet modem was as slow as molasses.*
b. *The clerks in that post office are as slow as molasses.*
c. *When her teenage son was mowing the lawn he moved as slow as molasses.*

As smart as a whip

When wielded with skill, the tip end of a whip moves with great speed, and can cause sharp pain; even cut like a sharp knife. Now, the expression also refers to someone who is very sharp-minded, very intelligent.

a. *The new sales manager is as smart as a whip!*
b. *Forget it, man! She won't date a guy unless he is as smart as a whip!*
c. *He came on as smart as a whip, but it was just an act.*

As smooth as silk

Everyone who has ever touched silk knows it is smooth, and immediately understands when something is compared with the smoothness of silk.

a. *The new wrinkle-free fabric looked as smooth as silk.*
b. *When Mike hits on a girl his come-on is as smooth as silk.*
c. *The politician was as smooth as silk*

As steady as a rock

People who are always calm, collected and in control of themselves and situations may be described as being as steady as a rock.

a. *A good leader should be as steady as a rock.*
b. *Those kids turned out well because their parents were as steady as a rock.*
c. *In business it helps to be as steady as a rock.*

As stubborn as a mule

Mules are notoriously stubborn, as are some people.

a. *Teenagers can be as stubborn as mules when it comes to accepting advice.*
b. *He finally succeeded because he is as stubborn as a mule.*
c. *Don't be as stubborn as a mule! It's for your own good!*

As subtle as an earthquake

Serious earthquakes are, of course, anything but subtle, so this saying refers to someone or something that is very conspicuous, very loud, often causing a lot of damage.

a. *A lot of today's TV advertising is about as subtle as an earthquake!*
b. *She's as subtle as an earthquake when it comes to talking about people.*
c. *Your comment was about as subtle as an earthquake.*

Asleep at the wheel

Doing things without knowing what you are doing; blindly doing business without noticing what is going on in the marketplace, may be referred to as being "asleep at the wheel."

a. *Between 1960 and 1980 American automobile manufacturers were asleep at the wheel, giving Japanese carmakers an extraordinary opportunity to win market share in the United States.*
b. *Some people go through life asleep at the wheel.*
c. *Wake up, man! You're asleep at the wheel!*

At all costs

"At all costs" is a colloquial way of saying that something is wanted no matter what it costs or how much effort may be required to obtain it.

a. *He was determined to get into that company at all costs.*
b. *I wanted it at all costs. It was a do or die situation.*
c. *Once she decided that she was going to marry him at all costs she went after him like a bear goes for honey.*

At heart

"At heart" refers to the inherent nature of a person, which may not always be obvious from his or her behavior.

a. *He acted callous and thoughtless but at heart he was really kind and thoughtful.*
b. *At heart, I never wanted to study math. I wanted to study astronomy.*
c. *His comments were insulting, but at heart I knew they were true.*

At stake

A stake is a piece of wood or metal sharpened at one end for driving into the ground, as a marker, a fence pole, or a tent peg. In earlier times, people were tied to stakes and burned as a form of execution. All of these meanings have come together in the term "at stake," in reference to something important that may be lost or gained.

a. *I knew my reputation was at stake.*
b. *There was a huge amount of money at stake in the project.*
c. *The union put its existence at stake when it went out on strike.*

At the drop of a hat

Hats, may of course, drop off your head without warning. This expression refers to doing something quickly, immediately.

a. *I would go out with that girl at the drop of a hat if I had the chance.*

b. *I would quit my job at the drop of a hat if I had a better offer.*
c. *That guy will start up a new project at the drop of a hat.*

Back down

This term comes from the concept of literally backing up in the face of danger of some kind, or backing down to avoid a confrontation or defeat.

a. *I refused to back down when the boss threatened to fire me.*
b. *If you back down now you will not be in any trouble.*
c. *No matter how serious the challenge, he never backs down.*

Back on one's feet

"Back on one's feet" has two common uses. In one it refers to returning to good health after some kind of injury or sickness. In the other use it refers to returning to a previous condition after a decline or failure of some kind.

a. *I was back on my feet two weeks after an operation.*
b. *He lost his job last year but is now back on his feet with a better job.*
c. *I will see you as soon as I am back on my feet.*

Back out

This phrase is derived from the physical action of backing up or backing out of a place for some reason, often to avoid some kind of danger. It is now used in reference to commitments of one kind or another.

a. *Once he makes a commitment he never backs out.*
b. *The company backed out of the deal before we got started.*
c. *If we don't back out now it will be too late!*

Back to the drawing board

Many projects require detailed planning that includes the use of drawings of one kind or another, giving rise to the expression "back to the drawing" board when a plan or project does not go well and has to be started again from the beginning.

a. *As soon as the project was launched I knew we would have to go back to the drawing board.*
b. *When the negotiations slowed down we started talking about going back to the drawing board.*
c. *Going back to the drawing board is a waste of time. Let's forget it!*

Back to the salt mines

In earlier times working in a salt mine was an unpleasant and often dangerous experience, resulting "back to the salt mines" become a common way to refer to unpleasant tasks that needed to be done. The expression has a humorous element.

a. *Well! Lunch is over! It's back to the salt mines!*
b. *If we don't get back to the salt mines we're never going to finish this job.*
c. *He refers to every chore as going back to the salt mines.*

Bad apple

In common usage, a bad apple is someone who behaves in an immoral, illegal or otherwise disruptive way.

a. *Avoid that guy. He's a bad apple!*
b. *There is almost always a bad apple in any group.*
c. *He turned out to be a bad apple and spoiled the party.*

Bad egg

A "bad egg" is an egg that has spoiled, become rotten, smells bad and is no longer edible. It is commonly applied to people who regularly misbehave and are frequently in trouble.

a. *The guy she is going out with now is really a bad egg.*
b. *The new employee turned out to be a bad egg.*
c. *That man is a bad egg so you should avoid him if you can.*

Ball is in your court

In tennis when the ball is in your opponent's court you can do nothing but wait until it is hit back to you. This concept is also used in reference to all kinds of personal and professional relationships.

a. *We have made our final offer and the ball is in your court.*
b. *You have to make the decision. The ball is in your court.*
c. *Since the ball is in your court, it's up to you.*

Ball park figure

This expression derives from trying to guess the distance a baseball goes when hit by a batter. It means a rough estimate; a rough guess.

a. *The contractor gave us a ball park figure for the cost of repairing the new building.*
b. *Never mind the details. All I want is a ball park figure.*
c. *His ball park figure turned out to be way below the actual cost.*

Banker's hours

In earlier times, banks generally did not open for business until at least 9 a.m. and sometimes 10 a.m., giving the impression that bankers did not work as long as other people. "Banker's hours" thus came to mean a short work day.

a. *I wish I could work banker's hours!*
b. *When that guy decided on his own to work banker's hours he was fired.*
c. *My wife doesn't really work banker's hours. She just works part-time.*

Bark up the wrong tree

When hunting dogs chase a squirrel or other wild game up a tree they will continue to bark at their quarry until a hunter comes or until they get tired and wander away. Dogs never bark up the wrong tree, but figuratively people do.

a. *The detective finally realized that he was barking up the wrong tree, and started looking for a new suspect.*
b. *When you want to place blame on someone be careful you are not barking up the wrong tree.*
c. *For the second time this week I was caught barking up the wrong tree with my suspicions.*

Be a sweetheart

Being generous, being kind; going out of your way to help, is often described as "being a sweetheart." This is a very personal way of asking someone to do something for you or for someone else.

a. *Be a sweetheart and go to the store for me.*
b. *Be a sweetheart and wash my car for me.*
c. *I've had enough of being a sweetheart! Do it yourself!*

Be blind-sided

To be blind-sided means that you have been defeated, disadvantaged, surprised, etc., by something that you couldn't or didn't foresee coming.

a. *I was totally blind-sided by the accusation.*
b *The negotiating team blind-sided me with a new proposal.*
c. *That lawyer almost always manages to blind-side his opponents.*

Be flush/feel flush

The old expression "feeling flush" referred to blood rushing to the face, giving one a hot, uncomfortable feeling. The new meaning of "feeling flush" has to do with money; with how much money you have on hand. "Being flush" means you have lots of money.

a. *The company executives were feeling so flush they began thinking about acquiring other firms to strengthen their position in the market.*
b. *Being flush is a lot better than being poor!*
c. *Everyone in our company feels flush, so the mood is really upbeat.*

Bean-counter

In earlier times, farmers, trades people and others had to count their produce and products by hand to keep track of them. This custom eventually resulted in the term "bean-counter" is applied people, especially accountants, who were obsessively concerned about numbers, from production costs and inventory control to sales figures.

a. *All of the managers in that company are bean counters!*
b. *Say what you will, every company needs dedicated bean counters.*
c. *I hate to negotiate with bean counters!*

Beat a dead horse

Repeat something over and over when it is useless; from the obvious fact that no matter how much one might beat a dead horse, it will not do anything.

a. *Asking your lazy brother-in-law to go look for a job is like beating a dead horse!*
b. *Stop spending time on that project! You're just beating a dead horse!*
c. *Trying to get him to do something is like beating a dead horse.*

Beat around the bush

Speak in ambiguous terms; talk in vague terms; probably from the idea of walking around a clump of bushes while hitting them with a stick to drive out game that may be hiding among them.

a. *All you ever do is beat around the bush! Why don't you come right out and say what you mean!*
b. *There you go again! Beating around the bush!*
c. *He beats around the bush for half an hour before saying anything worthwhile.*

Beat one's brains out

This rather odd but common expression means to tire yourself out by trying with all of your energy to remember something or figure something out.

a. *You've been beating your brains out all day trying to remember where you met him!*
b. *I sat there for an hour beating my brains out, but no luck.*
c. *Rather than continue beating your brains out, take a break and come back to it.*

Beat one's head against a wall

This very useful expression means to struggle to understand or to achieve something, and failing in the effort.

a. *You've been beating your head against a wall for hours. Give it up!*
b. *After beating my head against a wall for days I decided to get help solving the problem.*
c. *That professor expects you to beat your head against a wall!*

Beat your gums

This rather graphic colloquial expression refers to talking loudly and continuously.

a. *Will you stop beating your gums and let somebody else talk!*
b. *She beats her gums from morning to night!*
c. *He beats his gums for an hour but never said anything important.*

Bed of roses

A bed of roses is obviously something that is very attractive, very pleasant.

a. *For most couples, marriage is not a bed of roses.*
b. *You're making a big mistake if you think life is a bed of roses.*
c. *My new job was a bed of roses compared to the last one.*

Behind closed doors

Behind closed doors refers to some action or event that takes place in private, in secret.

a. *Most political shenanigans are hatched behind closed doors.*
b. *You never know what goes on behind closed doors!*
c. *The decision was made behind closed doors.*

Behind one's back

The expression "behind one's back" means to say something or do something without someone's knowledge, secretly, surreptitiously—figuratively, behind their back and therefore out of their sight.

a. *You might say that talking about someone behind their backs is the coward's way.*
b. *I knew there were rumors of all kinds flying around behind my back.*
c. *Anything that I would say behind your back I will say to your face.*

Below the belt

This expression may have developed from the sport of boxing, in which it is illegal to hit an opponent below the belt because of the danger of causing serious injury. It also refers to a comment or action that is unfair, cowardly or mean-spirited.

a. *Some politicians love nothing better than to hit their opponents below the belt.*
b. *Her comment was definitely below the belt but I ignored it.*
c. *He was not above hitting below the belt if it gave him an advantage.*

Bend over backwards

Bending over backwards is difficult and sometime a dangerous thing to do, resulting in the expression being used in reference to going to extremes to do something, to help someone.

a. *I want you to help me but I'm not asking you to bend over backwards!*
b. *I will bend over backwards to make sure you get it.*
c. *He bent over backwards to help her get the job.*

Benefit of the doubt

This saying refers to accepting what is said or what appears to be true without demanding absolute proof.

a. *I don't know anything about your background, but I will give you the benefit of the doubt.*
b. *The judge gave the defendant the benefit of the doubt.*
c. *She said she would give me the benefit of the doubt.*

Bet on the wrong horse

If you bet on the wrong horse you lose your money. This expression is now applied to other situations where a wrong or bad decision is made and you end up losing.

a. *When it came to the new product line-up, I bet on the wrong horse.*

b. *My choice for president turned out to be a bet on the wrong horse.*
c. *If you bet on the wrong horse you have only yourself to blame.*

Bet one's bottom dollar

Your "bottom dollar" refers to the last of your money. So if you bet your bottom dollar you don't have any left.

a. *Some visitors to casinos can't resist betting their bottom dollar.*
b. *I bet my bottom dollar that the new enterprise would make it.*
c. *It takes a lot of courage to bet your bottom dollar on a new company.*

Between a rock and a hard place

This expression refers to someone being caught in a situation where they have no easy, desirable choices.

a. *He was caught between a rock and a hard place when he was told that he had to accept a transfer to a subsidiary or take a big cut in salary.*
c. *When my girl asked me to go to the opera with her I was caught between a rock and a hard place.*
c. *The job offer with a raise in pay in a department I didn't like left me between a rock and a hard place.*

Between the devil and the deep blue sea

This refers to situations in which there are only two choices or alternatives and both of them are unpleasant or dangerous. It came into being because in the early days of ships, sailors had to make many choices that were dangerous.

a. *It's true that we are between the devil and the deep blue see but we must have a distributor.*
b. *Take your pick. It's either the devil or the deep blue sea!*
c. *There must be some alternative between the devil and the deep blue sea!*

Between you and me

The two main uses of this expression refer to keeping something secret from others, including disagreements or fights between the two people.

a. *Let's keep this between you and me.*
b. *Until we figure out how to do it let's keep it between you and me.*
c. *Let's keep this disagreement between you and me.*

Big cheese, big gun, big wheel, big wig

All of these terms are used in reference to someone who is very important, or who acts like he or she is very important, is high ranking, is in charge, etc.

a. *The new director was a big wheel in his previous company but is not so important now.*
b. *Who is the big cheese in that company?*
c. *I've never seen so many big wigs in a single company!*

Big fish in a small pond

A "big fish in a small pond" refers to a person who acts like he or she is far more important or successful than they really are.

a. *When he went back to his hometown he was treated like a big fish in a small pond.*
b. *If you continue to act like a big fish in a small pond you're going to get into trouble.*
c. *The last thing I wanted to do was act like a big fish in a small pond.*

Big head/swelled head

When a person begins to act like they are important, especially more important than they really are, it is said that they have developed a big head or a swelled head.

a. *When he was promoted to manager his head swelled up like a balloon.*
b. *He developed a case of big head when he hit the jackpot.*
c. *Don't invite that swelled head to our party!*

Bird's-eye view

Since birds fly, they have an overview of things below them. This gave birth to the expression "bird's-eye view," meaning a general overview of something.

a. *Tokyo Tower gives you a bird's-eye view of the city.*
b. *To see how city traffic flows you need a bird's-eye view.*
c. *Our survey of the market was intended to give us a bird's-eye view of how it functioned.*

Birds and bees

The way birds and bees act has long been used as a reference to sexual behavior when explaining human sexuality to children. It is used as an overall euphemism for sexual behavior.

a. *She told her daughter about the birds and the bees during the summer holidays.*
b. *He's still too young to be told about the birds and the bees.*
c. *I think the idea of "birds and bees" is silly and confusing to children.*

Birthday suit

This interesting expression refers to complete nakedness, to being nude, in reference to newborn babies.

a. *The little boy was running around the picnic site in his birthday suit.*
b. *When you go to a pool party at his house all you need is your birthday suit.*
c. *She startled the people at the party by walking out in her birthday suit.*

Bite the hand that feeds you

It is well known, of course, that if you try to feed wild animals held in captivity they might bite you, resulting in the expression "bite the hand that feeds you," referring to turning against or hurting a helper or supporter; repaying kindness with some kind of wrong.

a. *I didn't want to bite the hand that fed me by criticizing the company.*
b. *If you continue to bite the hand that feeds you your family will suffer.*
c. *It doesn't make sense to bite the hand that feeds you.*

Bite your tongue/bite my tongue

It is virtually impossible to speak while you are biting your tongue, thus "bite your tongue" means to refrain from talking or to stop talking. Likewise, "bite my tongue" refers to the speaker himself or herself not speaking.

a. *If all you can do is criticize you should bite your tongue.*
b. *When I heard his comments it was all I could do to bite my tongue.*
c. *The teacher told Johnny to bite his tongue.*

Black sheep in the family

Black sheep are relatively rare and are really conspicuous in a herd. A family member who is conspicuously different from other members, especially someone who habitually misbehaves, is commonly called a black sheep.

a. *I often refer to myself as the black sheep in my family.*
b. *Almost every family has a black sheep.*
c. *Who is the black sheep in your family?*

Blank check

If you ever receive a blank check that has been signed you can fill in whatever money amount you want, so it's a big deal. If your company gives you a blank check on setting up a new department, it means you can spend any amount of money without any more approval. It is commonly used to mean you don't have to ask permission to do something.

a. *I'm not asking for a blank check! Just give me a reasonable budget!*
b. *I have a blank check on all expenditures under $100.*
c. *It would be dangerous to give him a blank check.*

Blood is thicker than water

In business, politics and other situations, family ties often take precedence over all other considerations, giving rise to this adage.

a. *When it came to the president choosing his successor, blood was thicker than water.*
b. *Who did you expect him to choose? Blood is always thicker than water!*
c. *This company is never going to prosper as long as blood is thicker than water!*

Blue in the face

Turning blue in the face is a condition that results from lack of oxygen, and is therefore dangerous. This has led to the expression being used in reference to someone becoming very angry, very upset, and very emotional.

a. *He argued with the supervisor until he turned blue in the face.*
b. *I was so mad I felt like I was turning blue in the face.*
c. *I could see he was turning blue in the face so I shut up.*

Bog down

A bog is ground that is so water-logged that it is soft and mushy, and may also be called a swamp or marsh. It is therefore difficult to walk on because you sink down into the soft ground. This gave rise to the term "bog down," meaning being slowed down or stopped.

a. *As soon as the talks started they got bogged down on some small details.*
b. *The meeting was adjourned when it got bogged down.*
c. *If we take that approach all we are going to do is get bogged down.*

Bottom out

This expression refers to something that has been going down reaching its lowest point, beyond which it cannot go, and is commonly applied to the stock market and other market activities.

a. *A lot of people began to buy shares as soon as the stock bottomed out.*
b. *I'm waiting until the market bottoms out.*
c. *The market for blue jeans bottomed out, and then began rising.*

Brain drain

This provocative expression refers to educated and talented people of one country leaving for another country where economic opportunities are better, or they are returning to the ancestral homeland to help build the economy.

a. *For many years there was a brain drain from Asian countries to the United States, as people sought better economic opportunities and lifestyles.*
b. *In the first decade of the 21st century the United States began to experience a brain drain, as many Asians chose to return to their home countries.*
c. *Brain drain has become a new element in the economic well-being of countries.*

Bread and butter

Bread and butter were long viewed as basic foods that were important to sustaining life. This resulted in the phrase being used to describe other things that were of special importance to people.

a. *The voters are worried about bread and butter issues like jobs and taxes.*
b. *This is not a bread and butter issue. It is strictly politics.*
c. *If you are seen as taking the bread and butter away from them you will be in serious trouble.*

Break one's neck

"Break one's neck" is a way of doing all that can possibly be done; working as hard as you possibly can; making every possible effort.

a. *You don't expect me to break my neck for the kind of pay I'm getting, do you?*
b. *He promised he would break his neck to get the work done on time.*
c. *I broke my neck for you, and this is all I get?*

Break through

"Break through" has the obvious connotation of breaking down some kind of barrier like a wall to get "through" to the other side. The phrase is used in reference to overcoming some kind of difficulty and being able to proceed.

a. *The new computer chip allowed us to break through the price barrier.*
b. *We need a break-through if these talks are going to succeed.*
c. *He came up with a solution that resulted in a complete break-through.*

Breathe down one's neck

If you stand behind someone and or following them very closely it can be said that you are "breathing down their neck." The expression refers to getting very close to someone you are chasing, and watching someone very closely to check on what they are doing.

a. *My boss has been breathing down my neck all day, waiting for me to finish the report.*
b. *All day long I've had the feeling that someone was breathing down my neck.*
c. *I work a lot better without someone breathing down my neck.*

Bring home the bacon

In earlier times the men in families and in family groups were primarily hunters, responsible for bringing home wild game (meat) that they had killed. This custom resulted in the expression "bring home the bacon," meaning to earn a family's livelihood.

a. *By the time he was eighteen, he was already bringing home the bacon.*
b. *I'm so busying bringing home the bacon I don't have time for anything else.*
c. *Politicians like to be seen as bringing home the bacon for their constituents.*

Bring off

The original term "bring," meaning to take something with you, to carry or convey, has been expanded to include accomplish something successfully.

a. *No matter how hard you try you will never bring that off!*
b. *We succeeded in bringing off the deal without any problems.*
c. *He said he would pay me a fee if I helped him bring off the deal.*

Buckle down

In a reference to buckling one's belt around the waist, this expression means to give your complete attention to your work, some problem or some effort, and do your best.

a. *I told him to buckle down or ship out (leave).*
b. *We really had to buckle down to finish the job before quitting time.*
c. *Some young people really don't know how to buckle down.*

Budget squeeze

Something that is being squeezed refers, of course, to pressure begin applied against it. Depending on what it is, the pressure may prevent it from moving, make it smaller, etc.

a. *When the company encountered a budget squeeze, it started laying off workers.*
b. *We had to stop advertising because of a budget squeeze.*
c. *He did not anticipate the budget squeeze and was unprepared.*

Bug in one's ear

Anyone who has ever had a bug in their ear will appreciate this expression. It refers to a hint or suggestion that one hears about, usually unexpectedly, that you can't seem to ignore.

a. *He put a bug in my ear about the possibility of a new website.*
b. *Once he gets a bug in his ear he can't stop thinking or talking about it.*
c. *If you want to get him to do something just put a bug in his ear.*

Bug someone

Bugs (insects) of many kinds can be very annoying and distracting, giving rise to the expression "bug someone," meaning to annoy or irritate them.

a. *Stop bugging me! I have work to do!*
b. *Why don't you go bug someone else for a change!*
c. *All he does is bug the women in our department.*

Built like a brick shit-house!

Said of a woman who has a curvy, voluptuous, solid figure, this is not an expression that one would use directly to a woman or to people who might regard it as vulgar.

a. *She's sexy looking but I wouldn't say she's built like a brick shit-house!*
b. *The girls we met last night were built like brick shit-houses!*
c. *I want a girl who is built like a brick shit-house!*

Burning a hole in his/her/my pocket

Money that a person wants to or is likely to spend quickly, especially said of young boys who are not used to having money.

a. *That boy earned $10 mowing the neighbor's lawn this morning and the money is burning a hole in his pocket.*
b. *You act like that money is burning a hole in your pocket!*
c. *Let's spend it before it burns a hole in our pocket.*

Burning the candle at both ends

People whose lifestyle is fast and furious, if they drink to excess and engage in other excesses, may be described as burning the candle at both ends.

a. *He was obsessed with fast living, and burned the candle at both ends despite the dangers.*
b. *Man! You'd better slow down! You're burning the candle at both ends!*
c. *When I was young I burned the candle at both ends.*

Butter up

Try to get on someone's good side by catering to them, praising them, etc., from spreading butter on toast or something else to make it tastier, more desirable.

a. *No matter how much you butter up the boss he is not going to give you an extra day off!*
b. *She has him so buttered up he doesn't know what is going on!*
c. *Will you do it if I butter you up?*

Butterflies in one's stomach

This expression, no doubt derived from the way butterflies flit around, refers to feeling light-headed from anxiety, stress or worries of some kind.

a. *I had butterflies in my stomach when I walked up to the podium to give a speech.*
b. *She never gave any indication of having butterflies in her stomach when she performed in public.*
c. *If you get butterflies in your stomach, sit back, relax and meditate for a while.*

Buy off

This phrase is used in reference to money being paid or given to someone or some enterprise to bring about a change in their behavior;

especially when the changed involved is immoral or illegal.

a. *The land developer tried to buy the politician off but was not successful.*
b. *In some countries buying off bureaucrats is a common practice.*
c. *I tried to buy my wife off by telling her I would take her out for dinner but it didn't work.*

By a long shot

A "long shot" refers to just that—a shot with a gun or bow and arrow in which the target is far enough away that hitting it is questionable. This idiom has two common uses. One use refers to accomplishing something that was a big gamble; the other refers to accomplishing something in a very impressive manner, well beyond expectations.

a. *It was a long shot but I decided to take it.*
b. *He beat the other runner by a long shot.*
c. *I wouldn't call that a long shot. It was too easy!*

By the sweat of one's brow

When you work hard you are likely to sweat, thus the expression "by the sweat of one's brow," meaning by hard work.

a. *He built up the business by the sweat of his brow.*
b. *The sweat of one's brow is often more valuable than money.*
c. *Let's invest the sweat of our brows, and make this a successful project.*

Call the shots

In shooting sports, it is sometimes the custom to "call the shots," meaning the shooter is told when to shoot, or the shooter indicates what he intends to hit with the shot. It is now used in the sense of decision-making.

a. *In that company the vice president calls all of the shots.*
b. *It's your responsibility! You call the shots!*
c. *This is my project so I get to call the shots.*

Can of worms

A "can of worms," originally referred to live worms collected and put in a can for use as fish bait. Now it is used in reference to situations that are very unpleasant, disadvantageous or otherwise present a problem.

a. *The new contract was so complicated it quickly became a can of worms.*
b. *If you get involved with that company you will be opening a can of worms.*
c. *I knew I was in a can of worms as soon as I accepted the new position.*

Can't cut hot butter with a knife

Said of someone who is inept, incapable of doing anything right.

a. *That new guy hired yesterday couldn't cut hot butter with a knife!*
b. *Why didn't you tell me he can't cut hot butter with a knife?*
c. *He can't cut hot butter with a knife but at least he is honest about it.*

Can't cut the mustard

Some mustard are very strong and have to be "cut," that is diluted, before people can eat them. This apparently gave birth to using the phrase to mean that someone is or was incapable of doing something.

a. *The new ballplayer looked good but he simply couldn't cut the mustard when it came to getting on base.*
b. *Alice will be promoted as soon as the boss thinks she can cut the mustard.*
c. *When my boss told me I wasn't cutting the mustard I was shocked.*

Card up one's sleeve

The original meaning of this expression referred to card players hiding cards in their shirt sleeves as a way of cheating. At an appropriate time they would add the cards to those they were holding in their hands to give themselves a better chance of winning. Now it also refers to anything that is held back, not revealed, until a critical time.

a. *In negotiating it often pays to have a card up your sleeve.*
b. *Diplomats are famous for having cards up their sleeves.*
c. *No matter what the situation, my wife always has a card up her sleeve.*

Carrot and stick

This interesting expression refers to offering a combination of a reward (a carrot) and punishment (a stick) to influence someone's behavior. It goes back to the days when mules and horses were trained by giving them carrots when they behaved well and punishing them when they misbehaved.

a. *Some parents take a carrot and stick approach to bringing up their children.*
b. *Dictatorships often rely on the carrot and stick approach to controlling people.*
c. *The carrot and stick approach doesn't work with me!*

Carry the day

Carrying the day refers to an idea or an action that is the most valuable, the most successful, the most interesting, etc. that was proposed or occurred during the day.

a. *The foreman's idea for reducing manufacturing costs carried the day.*
b. *My proposal was greeted with applause but it failed to carry the day.*
c. *Just once I would like to come up with a plan that would carry the day.*

Cash cow

The fact that a cow keeps on giving milk day after day led to the expression "cash cow," which refers to a service or product that keeps money coming in day after day and is generally the most profitable item a company has.

a. *If you keep on looking for a cash cow the rest of your business may fail.*
b. *When we realized that we had a real cash cow we celebrated.*
c. *Companies with cash cows are in high demand by investor groups.*

Cash in on

This expression may come from the world of gambling where you "cash in" (turn in or exchange) your chips for cash. "Cash in on" means to make money from some opportunity.

a. *Successful sports figures often cash in on their popularity before they retire.*
b. *I tried to cash in on my acquaintance with him but it didn't work.*
c. *The company cashed in on the success of its new product.*

Caught in the act

Caught doing something—often something illegal, unethical, or embarrassing.

a. *I was caught in the act of taking an extra piece of cake.*
b. *His wife caught him in the act of playing around with another woman.*
c. *The thief was caught in the act by a surveillance camera.*

Caught red-handed

The term "red" has many uses. In this case, being "caught red-handed" means to be caught in the act of committing, or having just committed, a crime or some other kind of act that is considered illegal or immoral, including sexual behavior.

a. *The shopper was caught red-handed trying to steal some cosmetics.*
b. *He was caught red-handed going into a house of prostitution.*
c. *I was caught red-handed opening my Christmas presents early.*

Caught short

Being "caught short" refers to not having enough money to pay for something right when you need it.

a. *He claimed that I had caught him short when I asked him to repay a loan.*
b. *If you get caught short it's your own fault!*
c. *I got caught short at a restaurant and couldn't pay for my meal.*

Caught with his/my/your pants down

For many people getting caught unexpectedly with their pants down may be an embarrassing situation. This expression has been expanded to refer to both embarrassing situations and being caught unprepared (which can also be embarrassing).

a. *When I was called on in class to answer a question I was caught with my pants down.*
b. *I have noted that American businesspeople going to Japan are often caught with their cultural pants down.*
c. *If you don't want to be embarrassed don't get caught with your pants down!*

Cave in

A cave is a hollow area beneath the ground, usually with an opening to the outside. By their nature caves are subject to collapsing, to "falling in on itself," when they are undermined, giving rise to the term "caving in." Caving in is now used in a general sense in reference to people giving up whatever they are trying to do.

a. *The union forced the company to cave in to its demands.*
b. *Their negotiating team suddenly caved in and agreed to our terms.*
c. *Now matter how tough the going I am not going to cave in.*

Change horses in midstream

Obviously it can be both difficult and dangerous for a horseback rider to change from one horse to another in the middle of a deep and fast-moving stream. This resulted in the expression "change horses in midstream" to mean making a change in the middle of some important activity, such as bringing in a new manager.

a. *When they said they were going to change lawyers, I told them that they shouldn't change horses in midstream.*
b. *The directors decided to change horses in midstream, and dumped the CEO.*
c. *If things are simply not working out changing horses in midstream may be the best thing to do.*

Change of heart

The human heart is often equated with feelings and desires and other matters of the mind. When people have a "change of heart" it means they changed their minds.

a. *As soon as I saw the mountain I had a change of heart about climbing it.*
b. *When he was offered more money he had a change of heart.*
c. *When she offered to accompany me I had a change of heart about going.*

Chew the fat

This term probably relates to the fact that fried fat is very tasty, and used to be regarded as a special treat that people would chew for as long as possible to get the most out of it. Sitting around chewing fat thus become synonymous with sitting around chatting or talking about pleasant things.

a. *After dinner we sat around and chewed the fat for several hours.*
b. *When I meet my old classmates we spend a lot of time chewing the fat.*
c. *You guys had better stop chewing the fat and get to work!*

Chicken out

Chickens are not known for courage, so "chicken out" means to refuse to do something or to stop doing something out of fear.

a. *He was going to come with us on a river-float but he chickened out at the last moment.*
b. *Don't chicken out on me now! I told the girls you would come!*
c. *I knew you will chicken out!*

Chip in

A chip can be a small piece of something broken or cut off, a crack or another mark caused by chipping, or something very small, a disk or something used in the game of poker to represent money. If you "chip in" it means you contribute some money and pay for something jointly with others.

a. *I chipped in for a wedding present for her.*
b. *We all chipped in to pay for our company trip.*
c. *Everybody got mad at me when I refused to chip in.*

Chip off the old block

This saying refers to a son who is very much like his father, and derives from the similarity of chips cut from the same piece of wood.

a. *American President George W. Bush was a chip off the old block.*
b. *When someone describes me as a chip off the old block I consider it a compliment.*
c. *He'll never make it. He's a chip off the old block.*

Chip on his shoulder

In earlier times, fights used to be staged by one person putting a chip (a piece of wood) on his shoulder and daring another person to knock the chip off. If the other person knocked the chip off, the fight was on. Now, someone who has a short temper, is easy to anger, and quick to argue or fight is often described as having a chip on his shoulder.

a. *Chill out, man! You act like you have a chip on your shoulder!*
b. *I don't know why, but he always seems to have a chip on his shoulder.*
c. *If you go around with a chip on your shoulder somebody may knock it off.*

Choked up

One may choke on liquid, food or any kind of solid material. But in this case being choked up refers to be emotionally overwhelmed to the point that you cannot speak normally.

a. *When he heard the news of his son's death he became all choked up.*
b. *I got choked up when I was asked to give a speech.*
c. *Come on! It's no big deal! Don't get all choked up about it!*

Clam up

The use of the term "clam" is obvious in this expression, since clams close their shells when they are in any kind of danger. It means to stop talking.

a. *He carried on for nearly half an hour before he finally clammed up.*
b. *Tell those guys in the hallway to clam up.*
c. *She wouldn't listen to anything I said so I clammed up.*

Clean house

This expression obviously derives from the custom of sweeping and mopping homes. It is now commonly used in the sense of getting rid of unwanted or undesirable employees.

a. *The first thing the new owners did was to clean house. They fired every employee they regarded as unproductive.*
b. *If the new employees don't shape up the manager is going to clean house.*
c. *Let's clean house and start all over again.*

Clean sweep

An expression that derives from sweeping a floor or a place completely clean of all debris; now also referring to complete success, winning everything, the whole series, etc.

a. *The Giants made a clean sweep of the series.*
c. *The new owners are going to make a clean sweep of the old management.*
c. *We won every game. It was a clean sweep!*

Clean up

In addition to "cleaning up" something, this phrase is also used in the sense of making a lot of money very fast.

a. *He cleaned up at the horse races last year but now he's broke.*
b. *I had hoped to clean up with the new computer game but couldn't get it into the market.*

c. *Nowadays, it seems like the only people who really clean up in companies are top executives who vote themselves huge salaries and benefits.*

Clean your plate

I do not guarantee that the story of how this saying came into use is true. According to this version, the square plate (page 118) was never washed. After your meal of stew, you wiped the bowl-portion of the plate clean with a piece of bread. Then you flipped it over and used the flat surface for your dessert (if there was any). As time went by "cleaning your plate" came to mean eating everything on your plate as well as finishing everything. A related saying, "come clean," referred to revealing everything to someone.

a. *If you don't clean your plate you cannot have any dessert.*
b. *She kept insisting that I come clean about where I went last night.*
c. *I took too much so I couldn't clean my plate.*

Clip one's wings

It has long been common to clip the wings of some chickens or other domesticated fowls to prevent them from being able to fly over fences or fly away. If you "clip someone's wings" it means you do something to limit or control their behavior.

a. *The manager clipped the wings of the new salesman because he was too aggressive.*
b. *If you don't shape up I will clip your wings by taking away your driving privileges.*
c. *My wife clipped my wings when I began to talk about going on a golf trip.*

Close ranks

Originally a military term referring to a group of soldiers coming together in a close formation, "close ranks" now refers to any group uniting and acting as a team in order to strengthen its response to some challenge.

a. *The political party finally closed ranks and began an all-out campaign to win.*
b. *The coach warned the team members that if they did not close ranks and pull together they were going to lose.*
c. *Let's close ranks and give this project our best shot.*

Closing the books

Closing a book indicates, of course, that you are no longer reading it. This concept has been extended to refer to the end of a bookkeeping period or order taking period in business.

a. *When does that company close its books?*
b. *We close our books in March.*
c. *They won't consider any new business until they close their books.*

Clue in

This expression takes its meaning from "clue," which refers to anything that directs or guides one in the solution of a problem or mystery. If you "clue somebody in" it means you provide them with the information or intelligence they need for some purpose.

a. *The company failed because it was not clued in to the preferences of consumers.*
b. *Clue me in so I can get started.*
c. *We need somebody who is already clued into the market.*

Cock and bull story

This expression was originally a long animal fable about a cock (a male chicken) charging into a bull. It now refers to an absurd or highly improbable tale; and is similar to describing something as "bull-shit."

a. *People who are good at telling cock and bull stories are often popular.*
b. *That's a cock and bull story if I ever heard one!*
c. *How long are you going to stick to that cock and bull story?*

Cold call

A "cold call" refers to making a sales call on a person or company without having an appointment, the inference being that you might get a "cold" or unfriendly reception.

a. *I think Americans must have "invented" the practice of making cold calls on business prospects.*
b. *The "cold" sales call is still rare in Japan.*
c. *If you are going to make cold calls you had better be very good at "breaking the ice" in order to get your prospect to really listen to your sales pitch.*

Cold enough to freeze the balls off a brass monkey

This is a vulgar expression used by some when it is especially cold.

a. *Boy! It's cold enough to freeze the balls off a brass monkey!*
b. *Stay inside! It's cold enough to freeze the balls off a brass monkey!*
c. *New York in the winter can be cold enough to freeze the balls off a brass monkey!*

Cold shoulder

"Cold shoulder" refers to a cool or unfriendly attitude or behavior toward other people.

a. *I was afraid I would get the cold shoulder treatment when I joined the company.*
b. *When I met my girlfriend today she gave me the cold shoulder.*
c. *I was surprised to get a cold shoulder from my coworkers.*

Come apart at the seams

Pieces of fabric sewn together with weak thread are likely to come apart at the seams. People who experience some kind of shock may also lose control of their emotions and figuratively fall apart.

a. *When he told her he wanted a divorce she came apart at the seams.*
b. *When she started asking me questions I just came apart at the seams!*
c. *The thought of speaking in public made her come apart at the seams.*

Come clean

This is a request or an order for someone to tell the truth, to tell the whole story, about something.

a. *When he was first arrested he refused to come clean.*
b. *The teacher gave the student a chance to come clean but he refused.*
c. *I decided to come clean when it became obvious she didn't believe me.*

Come crawling back

Return in a very humble, obsequious way, usually after some kind of offense.

a. *When she accused him of being unfaithful he left in a huff, but soon came crawling back!*
b. *Just wait! He'll come crawling back before the end of the week!*
c. *I had to swallow my pride and go crawling back to her.*

Come hell or high water

This saying is based on the idea that high water (floods) and other hellish events are normally to be feared and avoided, but there are times when the dangers are ignored.

a. *Come hell or high water, I am going to take a vacation this year.*
b. *He said he was going to come hell or high water.*
c. *That guy never quits come hell or high water.*

Come-on

A seductive ploy to attract someone sexually, to sell a product, or to influence someone in some way that is not totally open or honest.

a. *Using pretty girls in skimpy clothes to help sell cars is a classic come-on.*
b. *You'd better tone down your lipstick! Red is a real come-on!*
c. *He has the best come-on in the business when it comes to meeting women.*

Come on like a brass band

Be loudly aggressive in conversation or in a presentation—a take-off on the noise made by a marching brass band in a parade.

a. *Look! You don't have to come on like a brass band! Just give me the facts!*
b. *The store clerk came on like a brass band.*
c. *Coming on like a brass band will get you nowhere.*

Come on like gangbusters

Gangbusters is a term that became popular in the United States in the 1930s, when the police and FBI began staging sudden, fast raids on gangster hideouts, busting down doors, and so on. "Come on like gangbusters" soon became synonymous with any sudden, aggressive action.

a. *The new CEO and his team came on like gangbusters, ordering dramatic changes in the way the company operated.*
b. *If we want to win we'd better come on like gangbusters.*
c. *The sales team came on like gangbusters and took the lead.*

Come on strong

"Coming on strong" means to be very aggressive in your approach to others, not only in language but in physical actions as well.

a. *The speaker came on so strong he angered the audience.*
b. *Most women don't like men who come on strong.*
c. *I'm looking for salesmen who come on strong but know how to do it without upsetting anyone.*

Come out on top

"Come out on top" refers to winning, to being first; probably from the sport of wrestling in which the one who ends up on top is usually the winner.

a. *If you want to come out on top you have to be more diligent.*
b. *No matter what the obstacles, he always comes out on top.*
c. *When those two argue she always comes out on top.*

Come to terms

Coming to terms refers to reaching an agreement in any kind of situation that is being discussed or negotiated.

a. *This meeting is not going to end until we come to terms!*
b. *You don't seem to be interested in coming to terms.*
c. *If you will just give a little we can come to terms in a few minutes.*

Come up short

This common expression is used when there is not enough of something—money, experience, skill, etc.

a. *Unfortunately, when he was promoted his talents came up short.*
b. *When I count my money I always come up short.*
c. *You need to study if you don't want to come up short in life.*

Come up smelling like a rose

When someone gets into a situation that looks like it is going to be very damaging to their success or reputation, and they emerge from it even better off than they were, they are said to have come up smelling like a rose.

a. *No matter what kind of trouble he gets into he always comes up smelling like a rose!*
b. *I thought I was going to lose everything but I came up smelling like a rose.*
c. *Some people can fall into bucket of do-do and come up smelling like a rose.*

Common ground

The original meaning of "common ground" referred to an area of land that was shared for some use. Not it generally applies to shared beliefs or interests.

a. If we cannot find some common ground we cannot work together.
b. We soon discovered that we had a lot of common ground with the newcomers.
c. Even though they behaved like enemies they had a lot of common ground.

Company man

A person who "buys into" (accepts) the philosophy of his company and is especially loyal to it is often called a "company man."

a. *My father was a strong company man.*
b. *You have to become a company man if you want to work for that company.*
c. *It may be hard for a real company man to change jobs.*

Company town

Towns in which there is a single company that employs most of the residents and dominates the economy is often described as a company town.

a. *Living in a company town can be limiting for young people.*
b. *When a company town loses its main source of employment it can be disastrous for the whole community.*
c. *There are many company towns in Japan.*

Complete washout

Washing or scrubbing something is done to remove dirt, stains and any other kind of matter that soils something. A washout refers to the erosion of a soft surface, such as a road. A complete washout has come to mean a complete failure; something that was cancelled.

a. *The concert was a complete washout. Nobody came!*
b. *My date was a complete washout!*
c. *The new product introduction was a complete washout.*

Cook one's goose

To "cook one's goose" refers to eliminating or destroying something that affects the actions and options of someone else.

a. *When I heard that I was going to be fired I knew my goose was cooked.*
b. *The employees cooked their own goose when they fought management and lost.*
c. *If the pilots continue to insist on higher pay they will eventually cook their own goose.*

Cook the books

"Cooking the books" is an expression that grew out of cooking food to make it taste better. It refers to illegally changing accounting information in the company books to make the financial situation of the company look better than it is.

a. *The accountant was cooking the books for over a year before he was caught.*
b. *The company went bankrupt after it was learned that its books had been cooked.*
c. *Some companies become very clever at cooking their books.*

Cool as a cucumber

It is necessary to keep cucumbers cool in order to preserve them over a period of days, and once cooled they stay cool for a considerable period of time because they are mostly water. It eventually became common to compare people who were typically cool and calm in their behavior with cucumbers.

a. *It doesn't make any difference what happens he is always as cool as a cucumber.*
b. *If you want to impress him you'd better stay as cool as a cucumber.*
c. *When I won the lottery I tried to stay as cool as a cucumber.*

Cool one's heels

This interesting expression refers to being forced to wait for an appointment, or for some other thing.

a. *I had to cool my heels for an hour before getting in to see the doctor.*
b. *Some people think nothing of forcing visitors to cool their heels for several hours.*
c. *I knew I would have to cool my heels for a long time so I took a book to read.*

Counting chickens before they hatch

Not all eggs necessarily hatch into chickens, thus this expression, which means you should not depend on make plans based on something before you get it.

a. *It is never a good idea to count your chickens before they hatch.*
b. *Don't count your chickens just yet! You may not get the job!*
c. *He is one of those people who go through life counting their chickens before they hatch.*

Cover ground

"Cover ground" is a colloquial expression that refers to talking about certain things, especially important facts or details of a situation.

a. *We have already covered that ground. Let's go on to the next topic.*
b. *Our team became impatient when the negotiators asked that we cover the same ground a third time.*
c. *We have only an hour to cover a lot of ground.*

Cover your ass

An extension of the concept of covering one's rear end (by wearing clothing), "cover your ass" now generally refers to taking steps to make sure you don't get blamed for something. It is a bit vulgar.

a. *The auditor is coming next week. You'd better cover your ass!*
b. *The only thing he is interested in is covering his ass.*
c. *It was the only thing I could do to cover my ass.*

Cover your tracks

Covering one's tracks is taking steps or measures to leave no trail that can be followed, generally to avoid being captured or caught in some undesirable situation.

a. *I tried to cover my tracks by making up a story.*
b. *He covered his tracks well but in the end he was caught anyway.*
c. *If we cover our tracks maybe we can get by with it.*

Crash course

A "crash course" is a study course that is very short and very concentrated.

a. *More business people should take crash courses in foreign cultures.*
b. *A crash course in a foreign language can be very helpful.*
c. *Taking a crash course in medicine does not make you a doctor.*

Crawl into a hole

Many animals crawl into holes to sleep, reproduce and escape from predators. People symbolically crawl into holes when they need to hide or when they want to escape unwanted attention.

a. *I was so embarrassed by her comment that I wanted to crawl into a hole!*
b. *Tell her to stop crawling into a hole every time somebody speaks to her!*
c. *When I failed the second time I just wanted to crawl into a hole.*

Crazy like a fox

Someone who acts dumb or foolish but is actually smart, from the practice of foxes to act strange or crazy to confuse or distract prey.

a. *He may act strange, but be careful! He's crazy like a fox!*
b. *He acts dumb but he is crazy like a fox.*
c. *Acting crazy like a fox can be an advantage sometimes.*

Cream of the crop

In a bottle or pail of pure fresh milk, the cream always rises to the top. Since cream is rich in taste and nutrients it has always been highly prized, resulting in the phrase "cream of the crop," meaning the best of a number of things.

a. *When hiring school graduates companies look for the cream of the crop.*
b. *The new employees were obviously the cream of the crop.*
c. *When shopping for vegetables she always looks for the cream of the crop.*

Crocodile tears

The eyes of crocodiles shed water, but they are not crying, so this phrase refers to someone who pretends to cry, shedding lots of tears, as a ploy to gain sympathy or to gain his or her way in some situation.

a. *The TV evangelist caught patronizing prostitutes immediately began crying crocodile tears.*
b. *Don't be a sucker! That was an act! She was crying crocodile tears!*
c. *You may as well stop it. Those crocodile tears don't impress me.*

Cross one's fingers

The act of crossing one's fingers to invoke good luck probably had some religious connotation in the beginning but it is now just an ordinary, and much used, expression.

a. *I'll keep my fingers crossed while you are interviewing for the job.*
b. *He kept his fingers crossed all the time but his team still lost the game.*
c. *Doing your homework will help you more than crossing your fingers!*

Cross that bridge when you come to it

You cannot cross a bridge until you come to it, resulting in the use of this expression in reference to not facing something too soon or before you have to.

a. *I know I have to pay my back taxes, but I will cross that bridge when I come to it.*
b. *She always tries to cross a bridge before she comes to it.*
c. *If you don't start now you won't be able to cross that bridge when you come to it.*

Cry wolf

People who lived in rural or forest areas used to be in danger from wolves, and a shout that a wolf had been seen was a warning to take seriously. Now when someone "cries wolf" it refers to a false alarm being given for some ulterior motive.

a. *The news media is always crying wolf about one thing or another just to attract readers.*
b. *The second time he cried wolf everyone ignored him.*
c. *If you are going to cry wolf there had better be a good reason for it.*

Cuss a blue streak

When people talk very fast without breathing for an extended period they tend to become blue in the face, apparently from lack of oxygen. So a rapid, lengthy stream of words came to be known as "talking a blue streak" or when the words were curse words, "cussing a blue steak."

a. *Today when some women get mad they cuss a blue streak.*
b. *She overhead him cussing a blue streak!*
c. *She cussed a blue streak for over an hour!*

Custer's last stand

This expression refers to the battle fought by American General George Custer against Indians at Little Bighorn in the Dakotas in 1876. He and all of his men were killed. Now, it is used to mean staking your job, money, or reputation, etc., on something that is doomed to fail.

a. *The man accused of fraud took a Custer's last stand approach and went down fighting.*
b. *It was a classic Custer's last stand! He never gave up even after he was defeated.*
c. *Look! Your "Custer's last stand" approach is crazy!*

Cut a deal

Cut means to penetrate something with a sharp edge, such as a knife. This meaning has been expanded to refer to penetrating (reaching) the heart of a matter and coming to an agreement.

a. *As soon as all of the details were on the table we were able to cut a deal.*
b. *It took us only a few minutes to cut a deal.*
c. *Executives from the two companies talked all day but could not cut a deal.*

Cut back

"Cut back" is a colloquial expressing meaning to reduce something, such as investment, number of employees, advertising budget, etc.

a. *As soon as I joined the company it cut back on its budget for entertainment.*
b. *Right after the merger cut back rumors began to circulate throughout both companies.*
c. *I promise you, no matter how tough things get I will not cut back on anything.*

Cut both ways

"Cut both ways" refers to something, a comment or an action that has opposing effects, often one positive and one negative.

a. *Complaining to my boss cut both ways. He was pleased that I brought it to his attention, but he was angry that I had waited so long.*
b. *Be careful what you say. It may cut both ways!*
c. *He really gets a kick out of making comments that cut both ways.*

Cut corners

This term refers to taking a short cut in a job or process, to doing less than is expected or is called for by the plans or specifications.

a. *The builder was sued for cutting corners in the construction of the bridge.*
b. *He is always looking for a way to cut corners.*
c. *There are no more corners we can cut on this job.*

Cut off

"Cut off" refers to stopping something as well as a predetermined time or date when something is set to end.

a. *As soon as she started getting personal I cut off the conversation.*
b. *The end of the month was set as the cut off date for completing the project.*
c. *Our communication was suddenly cut off without any explanation.*

Cut one's losses

Cutting losses means to reduce expenditures by taking some action, such as reducing salaries, reducing manufacturing costs, eliminating unprofitable products or marketing programs, etc.

a. *The first thing the new CEO said was that he was going to cut our losses in half.*
b. *We need to cut losses without reducing service to our existing customers.*
c. *CEO's who are really good at cutting losses are in high demand.*

Cut one's throat

The expression "cut one's throat" refers to some action that has very serious consequences.

a. *If you argue with the boss you will be cutting your own throat!*
b. *I tried to get him to transfer the troublemaker but I ended up cutting my own throat.*
c. *Don't cut your own throat just because you are mad at him.*

Cut some slack

Slack means loose, not tight, and in this case, cutting someone some slack means to give them more room or more opportunity to do things on their own; reducing the restraints on their behavior.

a. *He will never behave if you don't cut him some slack.*
b. *Some people work better if you cut them some slack.*
c. *I think you went overboard by cutting him that much slack!*

Dark horse

A "dark horse" is especially hard to see at night, and this may have been the source of the "dark horse" label that is attached to candidates for public office who are not known to the public and have little chance of winning an election.

a. *During the last presidential elections there were several dark horses who soon disappeared from the scene.*
b. *Our new product started out as a dark horse but a brief mention of it on a popular TV show made it into a success.*
c. *I'm the dark horse candidate you have not been hearing about, and I'm running for president!*

Dead duck

"Dead duck" refers to a person or people being in situations where there is no hope for anything good to happen, and something bad is going to happen.

a. *When the students were caught playing hooky from school they knew they were dead ducks.*
b. *When I saw the size of the wrestler I was to fight I knew I was a dead duck.*
c. *The product was a dead duck even before it was launched.*

Deadbeat

"Deadbeat" is a slang term for people who do not pay their debts. It also refers to a lazy person, a loafer who does little or nothing.

a. *He was a total deadbeat but he had a great personality and everybody liked him.*
b. *The government is making an effort to collect money from divorced deadbeat dads who don't support their children.*
c. *Some people are just naturally deadbeats.*

Deliver the goods

The original meaning of "deliver the goods" was just that—the ability or means to deliver goods to a destination. Now it also means being able to do something; to succeed in some effort or enterprise.

a. *The company needs a CEO who can deliver the goods.*
b. *Our new sales manager had a lot of promise but he has never delivered the goods.*
c. *I guarantee you, whatever I promise I can deliver!*

Dime a dozen

A "dime a dozen" is an expression that is used in reference to things that are very cheap—figuratively so cheap you could buy twelve of them for ten cents. The connotation is that the thing or person is of little value and easy to get.

a. *Used computers are now a dime a dozen.*
b. *People like him are a dime a dozen.*
c. *She got angry when he told her that girls like her were a dime a dozen.*

Dirty one's hands

Getting involved in something that is illegal, immoral or shameful is often referred to as "dirtying one's hands."

a. *I don't want to dirty my hands by getting involved in any kind of scam.*
b. *The politician dirtied his hands when he became involved in a questionable land deal.*
c. *If you dirty your hands you may never be able to run for public office.*

Discretion is the better part of valor

It is generally better to be careful than to be courageous and take unnecessary risks; a position that especially applies to major decisions that might have serious consequences.

a. *I decided to delay my complaint because I realized that in this case discretion was the better part of valor.*
b. *Rather than put my job in jeopardy I decided that discretion was the better part of valor.*
c. *He doesn't believe that discretion is the better part of valor, and does whatever he wants.*

Do-gooder

Some people are virtually obsessed with doing good deeds for others, sometimes to their own detriment, and are commonly called "do-gooders." The description may have a negative or a positive nuance, depending on the situation.

a. *My wife is such a dedicated do-gooder that I often have to ask her to stop.*
b. *He has to be the world's leading do-gooder!*
c. *Every family needs at least one do-gooder.*

Doesn't have a leg to stand on

Things cannot stand if they don't have legs. Arguments and propositions that are so weak they are doomed to failure may also be described as not having a leg to stand on.

a. *You don't have a leg to stand on, so you may as well stop complaining.*
b. *He doesn't have a leg to stand on no matter what he says.*
c. *She admits she doesn't have a leg to stand on, but doesn't want to give up.*

Dog-eat-dog

This is a phrase used in reference to situations where there are no rules, in which anything goes in the pursuit of success or victory.

a. *That company does business on a dog-eat-dog basis.*
b. *New York often seems like a dog-eat-dog place to newcomers.*
c. *The new boss has a dog-eat dog attitude.*

Dog days of summer

During the hottest days of the year, dogs typically lay around panting in order to keep their body heat down. Any period of time in the summer when things slow down may be referred to as "dog days."

a. *The dog days of summer are usually bad for both business and sports.*
b. *The only thing he wants to do during the dog days of summer is go to the beach.*
c. *Everything slows down during the dog days of summer.*

Doing her/his/my/your thing

This phrase is a response given by a person who is asked how he or she is doing, usually in reference to his or her work or profession. The nuance of the saying may be either neutral or positive.

a. *Thanks to his wife, he has been able to do his thing even though it wasn't profitable.*
b. *You do your thing and I'll do mine.*
c. *Many people are happy only when they are doing their own thing.*

Don't cry over spilt milk

Once milk is spilled it is usually impossible to recover it, and it makes no sense to try. The saying "don't cry over spilt milk" refers to doing something that has happened that cannot be changed.

a. *It won't do you any good to cry over spilt milk. You may as well forget it.*
b. *She has a habit of crying over spilt milk, and it really turns people off.*
c. *The only advice I can give you is don't cry over spilt milk!*

Don't give me any of your lip!

This is a colloquial way of saying "don't talk back; stop making excuses; just shut up; I don't want to hear anything more from you!"

a. *Don't give me any of your lip!*
b. *I don't want to hear any more of your lip!*
c. *All I said to her was don't give me any more of your lip!*

Don't kid yourself

In this expression "kid" means to mislead; so "don't kid yourself" means to avoid misleading yourself.

a. *If you think this project is going to be a winner you are kidding yourself!*
b. *I say again! Don't kid yourself about the potential of that kind of approach!*
c. *We have been kidding ourselves all along.*

Don't sweat it

Literally, don't work up a sweat over something. Figuratively, don't try too hard, don't get upset about it; forget about it.

a. *Don't sweat it. If we get it done by tomorrow that will be fine.*
b. *If you can't do it, don't sweat it. I'll get someone else.*
c. *Just saying don't sweat it isn't enough.*

Don't take any wooden nickels

Some time in the past, nickels, or five-cent coins, were carved out of wood as interesting artifacts. Of course, they had no real value—thus the saying, which means don't be fooled; don't let anyone take advantage of you.

a. *If you are going to negotiate a new contract, be sure you don't take any wooden nickels.*
b. *Remember! When you deal with that guy, don't take any wooden nickels.*
c. *No wooden nickels, thank you!*

Down and dirty

Some work requires that you get down on the ground, and get dirty in the process. "Down and dirty" refers to doing whatever is necessary to succeed at something, even when it involves using unsavory or even illegal tactics.

a. *Watch yourself! That guy gets down and dirty when the stakes are high.*
b. *We may have to get down and dirty if we want to win.*
c. *That company plays it down and dirty with its sub-contractors.*

Down and out

Having no money, no job, and no way of helping yourself.

a. *Many people who are down and out live on the streets.*
b. *In some cities there are thousands of people who are down and out.*
c. *Being down and out is a terrible thing.*

Down to the wire

"Down to the wire" originally referred to reaching the end of something, such as a race. Now it refers to running out of time.

a. *The election campaign was down to the wire, and we were behind.*

b. *The negotiations continued down to the wire but finally ended successfully.*
c. *Let's try not to go all the way down to the wire.*

Drag on

Dragging something along on the ground can be slow process, resulting in the phrase "drag on" to meaning something that was progressing very slowly.

a. *The talks between the lawyers dragged on for weeks.*
b. *How much longer is this going to drag on?*
c. *That company is notorious for dragging on their negotiations.*

Drag one's feet

"Dragging one's feet" refers to acting slowly and reluctantly.

a. *It was obvious from the way he was dragging his feet that he did not want the project to succeed.*
b. *If you don't stop dragging you feet we're going to miss our plane!*
c. *My wife is famous for dragging her feet. My daughter calls it "piddling," which means she just continues puttering around while everybody waits for her to get ready.*

Drag one's heels

The rather obvious meaning of "dragging one's heels" is to act slowly or reluctantly for some reason.

a. *If you don't stop dragging your heels we will never get done!*
b. *We knew they were dragging their heels in the hope that we could give up.*
c. *In today's business climate if you drag your heels in making decisions you may be left behind.*

Draw the line

A drawn line is often used to set the boundaries or the limit of something. The line may be a real line or a virtual line. It may also refer to stopping something.

a. *I had to draw the line on my daughter's spending.*
b. *The directors drew the line at talking about health benefits.*
c. *Some girls draw the line on kissing on the first date.*

Dressed to kill

"Dressed to kill" means that someone is dressed in a style that is designed to catch the attention and impress everyone—something that movie and TV stars do as part of their image.

a. *She was dressed to kill when I saw her at the sales convention.*
b. *If you're just going shopping you don't have to dress to kill!*
c. *I made up my mind that I would dress to kill in order to attract her attention.*

Drive a hard bargain

In this case, "drive" is used in the sense of negotiating in a very aggressive, uncompromising way in order to gain an advantage.

a. *He drives a hard bargain even in very minor matters.*
b. *They brought in a negotiator who was known for driving a hard bargain.*
c. *We have to drive a hard bargain if the company is to survive.*

Duck soup

Duck soup is very easy to make. You just put some pieces of duck in water and heat it to a boil. This has resulted in "duck soup" being used to describe anything regarded as easy to do.

a. *Don't worry about being able to do the job. It'll be duck soup!*
b. *Solving the problem was duck soup.*
c. *Everything is "duck soup" to that guy, and it makes me envious.*

Eager beaver

Beavers are known to be very hard workers, thus the expression "eager beaver" refers to people who are extraordinarily ambitious and hardworking.

a. *She is a real eager beaver and will do very well in this company.*
b. *What we need in this department is a whole bunch of eager beavers.*
c. *You certainly could not call him an eager beaver.*

Ear to the ground

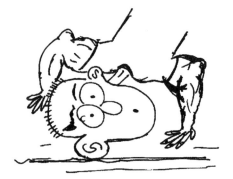

The ground carries sound remarkable well, and in the old days it was common to put one's ear to the ground to detect noises some distance away. Today, the expression refers to being attentive to everything that is going on around you in order to keep well informed.

a. *All during the conference I kept my ear to the ground for anything I could learn.*
b. *If you want to succeed in this company you have to keep your ear to the ground.*
c. *Keep your ear to the ground and your mouth shut!*

Earn a quick buck

"Earning a quick buck" refers to earning money quickly through some scheme or manner that is often a one-time deal. Such deals are sometimes illegal.

a. *They are only interested in earning a quick buck; not serving customers.*
b. *In that company earning a quick buck comes before quality.*
c. *I hear that John is looking for a way to earn a quick buck.*

Easier said than done

It is obvious that saying something is easier than doing it, giving rise to the use of this expression to suggest that doing something is more difficult that what it appears to be or is said to be.

a. *I can tell you one thing! Rock climbing is a lot easier said than done!*
b. *If you say that the job is easier said than done the boss will think you are not ambitious.*
c. *I know it's easier said than done but let's do it anyway!*

Easy come, easy go

It is human nature that when you have to struggle for something you value it more. In contrast, many people have a very casual attitude toward things they do not have to struggle for, particularly in the case of money.

a. *When he won the lottery he began to live by the easy come, easy go philosophy, and spent it all within a year.*
b. *Some people have an easy come, easy go attitude no matter how hard they have to work or how poor they are.*
c. *Your easy come, easy go attitude will get you into trouble!*

Eat crow

Crows have a bad reputation because they are scavengers that eat dead and decaying flesh, so the thought of "eating crow" is very distasteful to most people. The expression "eating crow" thus came to mean doing something very unpleasant.

a. *I made some big promises then I had to eat crow when I couldn't fulfill them.*

b. *You like to see me eat crow, don't you!*
c. *The president had to eat crow over his promise not to raise taxes.*

Eat one's words

The image portrayed by this expression is very clear. It refers to having to admit that something you said is not true, and you have to take it back by "eating your words."

a. *As soon as it was out of my mouth I knew I would have to eat my own words.*
b. *If you don't want to eat your own words you'd better be careful about what you say.*
c. *Time and time again I ended up having to eat my own words.*

Eat your heart out!

Envy, as is well know, can "eat" away at one's emotions until it makes them sick. This expression has to do with envy, but it is light hearted; not serious, and is normally said in jest.

a. *When my friend threw three strikes in a row, he yelled "eat your heart out!"*
b. *When my buddies began staring at my very pretty girlfriend, I couldn't resist. I said, "Eat your hearts out!"*

c. *I knew our new product would make our competitors eat their hearts out.*

Egg on

The word "egg" in this expression does not come from a chicken egg or any other kind of egg. It comes from an old Norse word meaning to encourage, to incite with dares and taunts or other comments.

a. *The rioting crowd was egged on by several people with loud speakers.*
b. *The players were egged on by their fans.*
c. *If we egg the manager on he might agree to support the project.*

Egg on one's face

This expression apparently came from the fact that people eating eggs would leave tidbits on their faces, indicating that they were sloppy eaters and didn't have good manners. It refers to an embarrassing situation.

a. *I somehow got mixed up and gave the wrong answer, ending up with egg on my face.*
b. *If you don't want to get egg on your face, you'd better make sure you're right.*
c. *I was as careful as I could be but still ended up with egg on my face.*

Face down

In the animal world it is common for opponents to attempt to intimidate each other by exhibiting a very aggressive manner, often with threatening facial expressions, giving rise to the expressing "face down."

a. *If we appear strong and relentless maybe we can face down the enemy.*
b. *The government decided to face down the striking transportation workers.*
c. *They faced us down without risking anything.*

Face value

The traditional meaning of face value is the value printed on a bill, a bond or something similar. It is now often used in reference to the apparent value or significance of something.

a. *The face value of a currency is often different from its purchasing value.*
b. *He said he would accept what I told him at its face value.*
c. *The sales value of rare things, like coins, may be well above their face value.*

Fake out

To "fake out" means to mislead someone into thinking you are going to do one thing, and then doing another, as in basketball.

a. *My company was really faked out by that false report.*
b. *He is very naïve and easy to fake out.*
c. *The runner who caught the football faked out all of the defenders.*

Fall flat on your face

This obvious reference to falling down and hitting your face has been extended to mean failing at something. As in: don't do it! You're sure to fall flat on your face!

a. *I tried to win by arguing but fell flat on my face.*
b. *Don't blame me if you fall flat on your face!*
c. *I was totally embarrassed when I fell flat on my face.*

Fall head over heels

This saying originated as a reference to falling in such a way that one turned a complete somersault. Now it is also used to mean totally, completely.

a. *The moment he saw her he fell head over heels in love.*
b. *He falls head over heels in love with every girl he meets.*
c. *Last night I fell head over heels in love.*

Fall through

This expression may have derived from falling through the ice on a lake or river that had frozen over. It is used in reference to scheduled talks that do not occur, plans that fail, or other things or events that do not happen.

a. *Their wedding plans fell through.*
b. *There was always the chance that the merger talks would fall through.*
c. *The deal fell through so we had to look for a new supplier.*

Falling into the lap of luxury

Suddenly becoming rich and living an affluent life is often described as "falling into the lap of luxury."

a. *He fell into the lap of luxury by winning the lottery.*
b. *Before the lottery the best way to fall into the lap of luxury was to marry it.*
c. *Many people dream of falling into the lap of luxury.*

Fast buck

A "fast buck" is money that is earned quickly and easily—and sometimes dishonestly.

a. *The company tried to make a fast buck on the property but they actually lost a lot of money.*
b. *He always jumped at every opportunity to make a fast buck.*
c. *We are not in the fast buck business, so we have to do it right.*

Fast money

"Fast money" refers to money that is, or can be, made easily and quickly, providing a kind of windfall—which is a sudden and unexpected piece of good fortune or personal gain.

a. *My cousin was more interested in fast money than in holding down an ordinary job.*

b. *If all you can think about is fast money you are not likely to make any money!*

c. *He has the reputation of being a fast money guru.*

Feather in one's cap

In the past American Indians wore feathers in a band around their heads as a sign of rank and prowess. Other cultures have also used feathers as head dressings. This practice gave birth to a "feather in one's cap," meaning something to be proud of.

a. *Getting a second degree from my university was a feather in my cap.*

b. *Winning the speech contest was a feather in his cap.*

c. *He has so many feathers in his cap that one more will not be noticed.*

Feather one's nest

Birds place loose feathers in their nests to make them soft and more comfortable. When a person "feathers his or her nest" it means they make themselves more comfortable financially, often by questionable means.

a. *High-ranking politicians are notorious for feathering their nests while they are still in office.*

b. *If you get caught feathering your nest you may go to jail.*

c. *I hope this new venture will help me feather my nest.*

Feel like a million bucks/dollars

It is easy to understand that having a million dollars would make you feel good. Thus if you "feel like a million dollars" it means you feel wonderful.

a. *When I heard the news it made me feel like a million bucks!*
b. *When the man won the lottery he said it made him feel like a million dollars, and then he smiled hugely!*
c. *It would be wonderful to feel like a million bucks all the time.*

Feet on the ground

People who have their "feet on the ground" are stable, sensible, and reliable.

a. *To make this work, we need to keep our feet on the ground.*
b. *Every team needs at least one person who has his or her feet on the ground.*
c. *If you want to succeed here you have to keep your feet on the ground.*

Fight tooth and nail

Most animals will fight with their teeth and claws when they are cornered. Since this expression applies to people rather than animals, it becomes tooth and nail. It means fighting as hard as you can, with all of the strength, skill and tactics at your command.

a. *The two boxers went at it tooth and nail.*
b. *We went at it tooth and nail with our main competitor.*
c. *Our backs were to the wall so we fought tooth and nail.*

Fill one's shoes

This expression refers to taking someone else's place, with the connotation that it will be challenging to perform as well as they did.

a. *I know I am replacing him, but I will never be able to fill his shoes.*
b. *You may not be able to fill his shoes, but do your best.*
c. *It is difficult to fill the shoes of a president who was as popular as he was.*

Fill the bill

"Fill the bill" used to mean filling an order for goods. It has since taken on the additional meaning of referring to something that is what is needed or wanted.

a. *The new pickup truck filled the bill where our transportation needs were concerned.*
b. *The new medicine the doctor prescribed for me filled the bill.*
c. *If it doesn't fill the bill I don't want it.*

Fine-tooth comb

The use of a "fine-tooth comb" has been expanded to mean paying special attention, taking great care in some effort so as not to miss anything.

a. *She went over my room with a fine-tooth comb looking for my credit card.*
b. *He always approaches every project with a fine-tooth comb.*
c. *We're going to have to use a fine-tooth comb to find the glitch in this software.*

Finger in the pie

People are always tempted to stick their finger into a pie to see what it tastes like. Now, having a finger in the pie also refers to being involved in something, like a business deal, for a profit.

a. *When the new deal closed I discovered that several outsiders had their fingers in the pie.*
b. *This project has so many fingers in the pie it may not be profitable.*
c. *Keep your finger out of my pie!*

First come, first served

A concept meaning the first in line gets served first, regardless of class, position, etc., a very democratic notion that is deeply embedded in the American psyche.

a. *One of the best things about America is the custom of first come, first served.*
b. *People really get angry if you ignore the principle of first come, first served.*
c. *We're all in a hurry, but it's first come, first served! So wait your turn!*

Fish out of the water

Obviously "a fish out of the water" is out of its element and in trouble. This expression refers to someone who does not fit in, is not capable of doing something, is unhappy, and may not last long in their present situation.

a. *I felt like a fish out of the water when I went to the party wearing blue jeans.*
b. *The new employee proved to be a fish out of the water when he tried his hand at selling.*
c. *You'd better prepare in advance if you don't want to be a fish out of the water.*

Fishing for something

"Fishing for something" means trying to find out something or trying to slyly get a compliment.

a. *I fished around in the car for several minutes, looking for my keys.*
b. *I kept fishing for a compliment about my new Italian suit, but everybody ignored me.*
c. *Ignore him. He's just fishing around, trying to get you to notice him.*

Fit like a glove

Something that "fits like a glove" is a perfect fit, and may refer to things as well as situations.

a. *The new job fit him like a glove.*
b. *After it was altered her new dress fits like a glove.*
c. *When the new members joined the team they soon fit like a glove.*

Flat broke

In this expression "broke" means to have no money. When you add "flat" to the expression it emphasizes that you have absolutely no money—not even a penny.

a. *Being flat broke is a scary feeling in today's world.*
b. *Every time he went to a pachinko parlor he came home flat broke.*
c. *The president of the bankrupt company paid all of his debtors, leaving himself flat broke.*

Fly by the seat of one's pants

This expression goes back to the early days of airplanes when pilots guided their planes by "feel" rather than instruments. It now refers to doing something by intuition or instinct rather than experience or prior knowledge.

a. *When we launched the new program we were flying by the seat of our pants.*
b. *I had to fly by the seat of my pants when my software developed a glitch.*
c. *Some people do better flying by the seat of their pants than others who have had a lifetime of experience.*

Foam at the mouth

When animals come down with rabies, they foam at the mouth, an expression that is now used to mean very angry.

a. *He became so angry he was virtually foaming at the mouth.*

b. *Watch it! He's about ready to foam at the mouth!*
c. *I felt like foaming at the mouth.*

Follow through

It is said that the "follow through" is the key to becoming or being a good golf player. "Following through," in any action that is undertaken is often critical to its success.

a. *Failure to follow through after negotiating a deal doesn't make any sense.*
b. *If you don't follow through with your promise your reputation will be ruined.*
c. *He said he would follow through but he didn't.*

Fool around

Doing things in a casual, non-serious way; also having sex with someone other than your spouse.

a. *One of the reasons for the high divorce rate is that many husbands and wives fool around.*
b. *All that new guy does is fool around.*
c. *He started fooling around when his wife left on a trip.*

Foot the bill

"Footing the bill" means paying the bill or the cost of something.

a. *I agreed to foot the bill for my wife's visit to a spa.*
b. *My company has agreed to foot the bill for me to take a refresher course.*
c. *I'm sorry, I'm not in a position to foot the bill this time.*

For a song

The expression "for a song" refers to buying something at a very low price—a reference to the fact that in earlier times songs were free.

a. *Some people get rich by buying old homes for a song, fixing them up, and selling them at a high price.*

b. *The store is going out of business so the owner is selling everything that is left for a song.*
c. *My brother-in-law always manages to buy everything for a song.*

For the birds

Birds eat things people don't normally like (worms and bugs), thus the expression "for the birds," refers to something that is not enjoyable, not likeable, not desired.

a. *The movie we went to see was for the birds.*
b. *That meal was for the birds!*
c. *I told the boss that his raise-in-pay offer was for the birds.*

For what it's worth

This saying is often used as a preface to a comment or statement that may not be needed or expected, and is something extra tossed in just in case it will help the situation at hand.

a. *For what it's worth, I will be in Tokyo next month and we can talk about it face-to-face.*
b. *Well, for what it's worth, I don't understand you either!*
c. *Sure my word is good... for what it's worth.*

Force one's hand

In earlier times it was important to know if a potential enemy had a weapon in his hand, resulting in the showing of any empty hand becoming a friendly greeting. "Forcing one's hand" thus became a protective measure.

a. *The negotiators tried to force our hand in an effort to get us to reveal our position early.*
b. *I wasn't ready, but they forced my hand.*
c. *You should be very careful when trying to force their hand.*

Fork over

This slang-like expression is an extension of the use of the common eating utensil (fork), and means to pay as well as to hand over. The connotation of the phrase is slightly negative.

a. *I had to fork over a lot of money for that painting.*
b. *I didn't really appreciate it when I had to fork over money for the bill.*
c. *The mugger ordered me to fork over my wallet.*

Gain ground

Originally a military term, gain ground is now also used in the sense of making progress in business and other endeavors, including overcoming some kind of serious illness.

a. *The hospital said his condition was still serious but that he was gaining ground.*
b. *A month after our start-up company was launched it began to gain ground in the market.*
c. *If we don't gain any ground by the end of the month, let's call it quits.*

Get a break

"Get a break" refers to getting an advantage of some kind, usually unexpected and unplanned.

a. *We got a big break when the value of the currency went up.*
b. *He got a break when he accidentally met the sales manager at a reception.*
c. *If we don't get some kind of break this project is not going to fly.*

Get a green light

A green light is widely used as a signal that means go or proceed, in the movement of vehicles as well as other situations.

a. *The new sales program got a quick green light from the manager.*
b. *It took me over a month to get a green light for my new project.*
c. *We couldn't start until we got a green light.*

Get a pink slip

In the past, employees who were being fired were given notice in writing on a piece of paper that apparently was pink in color, thus the expression "pink slip," referring to termination from a job.

a. *I received a pink slip last week and am now looking for a new job.*
b. *Everyone in the section got a pink slip on the same day.*
c. *The attitude of the manager made me think I would soon be getting a pink slip.*

Get behind a person or something

When you want to help someone move forward or push something forward it may be necessary to get behind them, thus "getting behind" a person or thing has come to mean giving help or support.

a. *When my friend announced that he was running for office, I promised to get behind him.*
b. *Several managers in the company refused to get behind the new project.*
c. *Don't worry! I'll get behind you.*

Get behind the wheel

Driving a vehicle requires that you get behind the wheel. This expression is now used in reference to starting a major push to introduce a new product, to extend extra effort to grow a product line or company, or to put extra effort into any project.

a. *The manager sent out a memo asking everybody to get behind the wheel.*
b. *The new CEO wasted no time in getting behind the wheel.*
c. *If you want to do well in school you have to get behind the wheel.*

Get cold feet

"Getting cold feet" refers to a loss of nerve or courage, which often leads to not following through on something.

a. *My wife and I planned to go to Europe but we got cold feet and decided not to go.*
b. *When my friend offered to take me flying in a glider I got a case of cold feet.*
c. *Management got cold feet and cancelled the marketing program.*

Get down to brass tacks

The history of this expression is unclear. It may be that making use of brass tacks in some work was the final step in the process and therefore of special importance. In any event, "getting down to brass tacks" means to begin the most important work or business, to "get down" to the heart of a matter.

a. *The talks were dragging on so my boss said, "Let's get down to the brass tacks."*
b. *I wanted to get down to brass tacks but my girl wasn't interested in getting serious.*
c. *He simply refuses to get down to brass tacks.*

Get down to business

"Get down" in this usage means to start, to begin, especially to be more aggressive in whatever activity you may already be engaged in.

a. *All right, everybody! It's time to get down to business.*
b. *If we don't get down to business we're never going to finish.*
c. *The new manager had a "get down to business" attitude.*

Get hold of yourself!

Get control of your emotions, your nerves; calm down.

a. *If you want to win this tournament you'd better get hold of yourself!*
b. *I knew I had to get hold of myself or fall flat on my face.*
c. *She got hold of herself and performed like a professional.*

Get it on

This expression may derive from the fact that a slang term for the erect male penis is "hard on." It is used in the sense of having sex with someone.

a. *He tried his best to get it on with her but she wasn't having any!*
b. *Did you get it on with him?*
c. *No matter how hard we tried we just couldn't get it on.*

Get my/your groove back

This phrase could have derived from the game of bowling, as when your ball is released in the right "groove" it will result in a strike. It refers to getting your act together, getting things done, getting in control of your life, getting the most out of life.

a. *After he lost his job it took him a year to get his groove back.*
b. *She took a long vacation from work in the hope of getting her groove back.*
c. *You'll never get your groove back if you continue doing the old things.*

Get off my back!

Carrying a child or a pack on your back is cumbersome and tiring, thus the expression, get off my back. It means stop pestering me, stop bothering me, stop criticizing me, and leave me alone.

a. *If you don't get off my back I'm going to punch you in the nose!*
b. *There is no way I'm going to help you, so you might as well get off my back!*
c. *It took weeks, but I finally got him off my back.*

Get off on the wrong foot

"Getting off on the wrong foot" refers to making a bad start when you meet someone or when you start something. The saying is probably a take-off on the military practice of having assembled troops step off with their left foot when they begin a march.

a. *When we first met he took something I said wrong, so we got off on the wrong foot.*
b. *It became obvious few days after we started the project that we had got off on the wrong foot.*
c. *Once you start off on the wrong foot it can be hard to recover.*

Get off the ground

Getting something off the ground means that, like an airplane, it has been successfully launched.

a. *We were just getting the project off the ground when we ran out of money.*
b. *Our goal was to get the project off the ground by the end of the month.*
c. *When we got the new product off the ground we held a celebration.*

Get on a high horse

Getting on a horse that is especially high, which puts one "above" others, has become an expression that means to behave with arrogance or with a sense of superiority.

a. *Every since he got promoted he has been on a high horse.*
b. *He is going to fall off that high horse one of these days.*
c. *I would like to get on a high horse at least once and give everybody orders.*

Get on the bandwagon

A bandwagon was originally a colorfully decorated wagon that carried members of a band in a parade. The phrase is also used to mean a cause or a party that attracts a lot of followers.

a. *As soon as the senator said he was going to run for the presidency many people rushed to get on the bandwagon.*
b. *That company always tries to get on the bandwagon of hot new products.*
c. *If you want to succeed in politics get on the band wagon of a winner.*

Get one's feet wet

"Getting one's feet wet" refers to doing something for the first time, or just starting out on some project.

a. *We won't know if it is going to work or not until we get our feet wet.*
b. *When it came to getting my feet wet with computers I was really intimidated.*
c. *Go ahead! Get your feet wet! You may like it!*

Get the upper hand

"Getting the upper hand" in any contest or endeavor means you achieve an advantage or victory.

a. *In the second half of the football game our team got the upper hand.*
b. *The union soon had the upper hand in its negotiations with the company.*
c. *We must make every effort to get the upper hand in the market.*

Get through one's head

"Getting through one's head" means to finally make them understand something or believe something.

a. *No matter how I explained it I simply could not get through his head.*
b. *It's very simple! Can't you get it through your head?*
c. *I couldn't get it through the bank manager's head that I didn't want to borrow any more money.*

Get to first base

In a baseball game you cannot score without getting to first base, thus "getting to first base" has come to mean making a good start in anything, including "making out" with a girlfriend or boyfriend.

a. *We started the project weeks ago but are not yet at first base.*
b. *The union and management announced that they had finally reached first base.*
c. *Did you get to first base with your new girlfriend?*

Get to the bottom of

Understanding what is going on, or the cause of something, often entails learning all of the details, and having to "dig deep" to get them—thus "get to the bottom of" something refers to finding out everything there is to know about something.

a. *I will make a decision as soon as I get to the bottom of what's going on.*
b. *He tried, but he couldn't get to the bottom of her problems.*
c. *The government often fails to get to the bottom of problems.*

Get to the heart of it

The heart is one of the most important organs in the body, so if you "get to the heart" of something it means you have gotten to the most important part or detail.

a. *After days of testing, we finally got to the heart of the trouble.*
b. *No matter how long he talked he never got to the heart of his subject.*
c. *I'll get back to you as soon as I get to the heart of the problem.*

Get under one's skin

Obviously something under your skin can be irritating or painful, thus the expression, "get under one's skin," means to bother them, to upset them, to make them angry.

a. *All of that noise is getting under my skin.*
b. *Your constant complaining is getting under my skin.*
c. *If you don't want me to get under your skin get your act together and do something worthwhile!*

Get what's coming to you/him/her

Be punished or suffer some loss because of your own bad actions.

a. *It may be sad, but you got what was coming to you.*
b. *Well, he finally got what was coming to him!*
c. *She got what was coming to her.*

Get your act together

Do things in a more effective manner; do things right, with the right attitude, the right approach.

a. *My boss told me that if I didn't get my act together he was going to fire me.*
b. *She finally managed to get her act together, and is now doing great.*
c. *If you can't get your act together you might as well leave.*

Get your ass in gear!

Vehicles have to put "in gear" before they will move, giving birth to the expression: "Get your ass in gear"—a rather vulgar way of telling someone to be more energetic, more effective, in their efforts.

a. *If you don't get your ass in gear you're going to be fired!*
b. *You'd better get your ass in gear and get it done today!*
c. *I don't know why but I just can't get my ass in gear!*

Getting a square meal

In earlier times dinner plates in Great Britain were often square pieces of wood with the center carved out to create a bowl to hold the various ingredients. People who traveled often took their "squares" with them. A "square meal" became equated with a full meal.

a. *Boy! That was a square meal!*
b. *Your wife really serves square meals, doesn't she!*
c. *Let's go where we can get a square meal. I'm really hungry.*

Getting tanked

When you drank too much out of the "tankard" (page 167) you were said to be "tanked". If you got so "tanked" that you passed out, there was a chance that somebody might think you had actually died. Since back then they didn't have experience with taking pulses, they often buried people alive who were actually in a drunken stupor or otherwise comatose. In earlier times British sailors in particular often got tanked.

a. *Some students think there is no harm getting tanked.*
b. *That man got so tanked last night he went to sleep on the sidewalk.*
c. *I've only been tanked twice in my life.*

Gift of the gab

"Gab" is a slang term for talking smoothly and excessively, especially about matters of little importance. Some people have a gift for gabbing, meaning they are very good at it.

a. *People who have a gift of the gab are often attracted to jobs in sales.*
b. *His wife has a gift of the gab that you wouldn't believe!*
c. *Why don't you make use of your gift of the gab instead of bugging people?*

Give an inch and he will take a mile

This expression refers to the behavior of aggressive people who always try to get more than what is offered or given to them. In most cases, it is a criticism of such behavior.

a. *Be careful what you give him. If you give him an inch he will take a mile!*
b. *Many children push the limit. When you give them an inch they will try for a mile.*
c. *I gave him an inch and sure enough he went for a mile!*

Give-and-take

This literally means to give something in exchange for getting something, and is, or course, a fundamental part of maintaining harmonious relationships with others.

a. *Right from the beginning we had a give-and-take relationship.*
b. *He is so selfish he doesn't know what a give-and-take relationship is.*
c. *After a lot of give-and-take we finally reached an agreement.*

Give as good as you get

In boxing, or any kind of fight, physical or verbal, if you are able to hold your own with an opponent in the exchanges, it may be said that you are able to give as good as you get. In other words, fight back or talk back with equal force.

a. *If you can't give as good as you get, you better avoid arguing or fighting.*
b. *I didn't win, but I gave as good as I got.*
c. *I had a run-in with my boss but I gave as good as I got.*

Give ground

This is another old military term that refers to moving back, giving up ground, to an enemy. Now, it is used in a general sense to mean weakening your position; retreating from a previously held position.

a. *In the face of his argument I had to give ground.*
b. *The negotiators tried every trick in the book to force us to give ground.*
c. *It seems that politicians are always willing to give ground in exchange for something else.*

Give in

Give in is similar to give up, in the sense that both mean to stop arguing, stop fighting, stop resisting. The additional connotation of "give in" is that it suggests you will do what the other person or party wants.

a. *I was surprised when she gave in.*
b. *If you will give in on this point I will make it up to you (give you something in return).*
c. *His political opponent gave in at the last moment and joined forces with him.*

Give someone a piece of one's mind

If you give someone a piece of your mind it means you tell them what you really think in a forceful manner, or you scold them angrily.

a. *I gave the store manager a piece of my mind when I told him about the faulty product.*
b. *He finally became impatient and gave the clerk a piece of his mind.*
c. *It took a lot of self-control to not give the shouting striker a piece of my mind.*

Glad hand

"Glad hand" refers to meeting and greeting someone excessively warmly and enthusiastically. An overdone friendly handshake can be called a "glad hand." Generally, a "glad hand" kind of greeting is regarded as insincere, and sometimes as offensive.

a. *The politician spent all day glad handing the crowd at the shopping center.*
b. *I was put off by the glad hand manner of the salesman.*
c. *If you want to make a good impression, it is better not to go around glad handing people.*

Gleam in his/her eye

Something that hasn't happened yet but is greatly desired and is being energetically pursued. Also, a "look" that one may have after achieving some outstanding success.

a. *Every time he saw her he got a gleam in his eye.*
b. *When you look at that new car you get a gleam in your eye!*
c. *The thought of winning the lottery puts a gleam in his eye.*

Glutton for punishment

People who never give up in their work on in strenuous sports activity, who work and play harder than expected and never complain are commonly described as being gluttons for punishment.

a. *My father was a glutton for punishment. He never quit; never gave up, no matter how hard the work.*
b. *My wife is a glutton for punishment.*
c. *Don't be a glutton for punishment. You shouldn't work so hard!*

Go back on your word

"Going back on your word" means failing to keep your word. In other words, breaking a promise or commitment.

a. *I was really disappointed when she went back on her word.*
b. *If you go back on your word you will be in trouble!*
c. *When it's time to sign the contract the company went back on its word.*

Go for broke

"Going for broke" means risking everything in some major action that is usually very important.

a. *We decided to go for broke, come hell or high water!*
b. *It seems that company is always going for broke on everything they do.*
c. *After going for broke at the meeting we finally reached an agreement.*

Go jump in the lake

This saying is used to inform someone that you are refusing to accept or to do whatever they have told or ordered you to do.

a. *Imagine my surprise when the girl told me to go jump in the lake.*
b. *When my boss told me to work overtime I told him to go jump in the lake.*
c. *When I asked him to help me he told me to go jump in the lake.*

Go like greased lightning

Greasing a wheel, for example, allows it to turn faster, so adding "greased" to lightning, which is already very fast, just emphasizes the concept of speed.

a. *The new product took off like greased lightning.*
b. *When the door opened the waiting shoppers went in like greased lightning!*
c. *When we got to the park the kids headed for the swings like greased lightning.*

Go over like a lead balloon

A balloon made out of lead is obviously not going to go anywhere, thus this expression, which means that the idea, project, proposal, etc. did not get a positive response; was not accepted.

a. *The suggestion that we look for a partner went over like a lead balloon.*
b. *The new product went over like a lead balloon.*
c. *As soon as I heard the proposal I knew it would go over like a lead balloon.*

Go to one's head

When something "goes to your head" it means you become proud and begin thinking and acting like you are better than others, that you are suddenly very important.

a. *When he got a promotion it went to his head, and he became overbearing.*
b. *Don't let hitting the jackpot go to your head.*
c. *When I came in first in the contest it went to my head.*

Going to hell in a basket

Baskets have traditionally been used to carry things when people went from one place to another, giving birth to this expression. It means doing things that will lead to a dangerous, maybe fatal outcome.

a. *If you get hooked on drugs you will be going to hell in a basket.*
b. *If he keeps that up he will surely go to hell in a basket.*
c. *The last time I saw him he was going to hell in a basket.*

Gravy train

In many Western cuisines, gravy (a sauce made by thickening and seasoning juices that drip from cooking meat) is a popular dish, giving rise to a number of additional meanings and uses for the term. One such meaning is "money." A "gravy train" refers to a job or occupation that requires very little effort or work, while yielding considerable profit.

a. *The new job turned out to be a gravy train for my brother.*
b. *If we can make this product a success it will be a real gravy train.*
c. *You may as well forget it. You are not going to get on a gravy train.*

Grease one's palm

"Grease" has commonly used to make things run more smoothly, particularly such things as wagon wheels. "Greasing someone's palm" means to pay for a special favor or to bribe them into doing something for you. It may be used in either a negative or positive sense, depending on the situation.

a. *If you want him to do anything you have to grease his palm.*
b. *In some areas border guards expect you to grease their palms.*
c. *Somebody is always greasing the palms of politicians.*

Green

In addition to referring to a young plant or fruit that is still green, this term is now used to describe a person who is immature and inexperienced.

a. *Every member of the new team is green, so nobody expects it to do very well.*
b. *It was quickly obvious that the new employee was totally green.*
c. *He may be green but he is very smart and ambitious and will make a good employee.*

Growth train

This is a relatively new expression that refers to a patent, product or service that has the ability to "grow" a company rapidly and continuously.

a. *The new video player turned out to be a growth train for the company.*
b. *A team was created to study how we could develop a growth train.*
c. *From now on, most so-called growth trains are going to come out of new technology.*

Half-baked

The cooking term "half-baked" is used in reference to plans or ideas that are not fully thought out or not fully developed.

a. *If you keep bringing half-baked ideas to the manager you will never get anywhere.*
b. *His plan was so half-baked it was laughable.*
c. *His professor told him his master's thesis was half-baked.*

Hammer out

"Hammer," of course, refers to a device used for pounding, as well as the act of pounding. "Hammer out" refers to working very hard to achieve an agreement—virtually "hammering" the different requirements or points until they are "down" and agreeable to both sides.

a. *The negotiations lasted all night but we finally hammered out an agreement.*
b. *Hammering out the details of the agreement took weeks.*
c. *Look! We can hammer this out! Let's not give up!*

Handle with kid gloves

"Kid gloves" are gloves made from the leather of young animals and is therefore very soft. The expression "handle with kid gloves" means to handle softly, gently, carefully.

a. *It is important to handle kindergarten children with kid gloves.*
b. *He handled the new employees with kid gloves for the first few days.*
c. *That customer is very important to us so handle him/her with kid gloves.*

Hand-over-fist

The colloquial expression "hand-over-fist" refers to large amounts of money coming in very fast.

a. *From the first day the shop opened the money came in hand-over-fist.*
b. *The hand-over-fist response we were expecting did not happen.*
c. *When the first MacDonald's opened in Tokyo the money poured in hand-over-fist.*

Hang-dog expression

This is a sad, dejected, sorrowful look on the face that some people use as a way of gaining sympathy.

a. *If you go around with a hang-dog expression people are going to avoid you!*
b. *Why the hang-dog expression?*
c. *That hand-dog expression is not going to get you anywhere.*

Hang in the balance

When two things hang in the balance, they might go either way if they become unbalanced. Thus, when something hangs in the balance there is an element of doubt, of uncertainty about the outcome.

a. *The outcome of the election hung in the balance until the last hour.*
b. *When we quit for the day the negotiations were still hanging in the balance.*
c. *Let's not leave this hanging in the balance!*

Hanky panky

This is a term that refers to devious or mischievous conduct, and is often used in reference to extra-marital sexual affairs.

a. *You think engaging in hanky panky is a male right, don't you!*
b. *I'm beginning to think John is up to some kind of hanky panky.*
c. *He says a little hanky panky is good for you.*

Happy as a lark

This saying refers to someone who is very happy, and behaves as if they could sing with joy.

a. *When she got the good news she was happy as a lark.*
b. *Sam just got promoted and is as happy as a lark.*
c. *I will be as happy as a lark if you say yes.*

Hard nut to crack

Some nuts are especially hard to crack open, thus the use of the expression "hard nut to crack" to mean something that is difficult to do, or some person who is hard to understand.

a. *The problem turned out to be a very hard nut to crack.*
b. *The new man was so passive and quiet that he was a hard nut to crack.*
c. *If you have a problem that is really hard to crack give it to John.*

Hard sell

An approach to selling something or some idea that is very aggressive, very direct, often to the point of being obnoxious.

a. *In the past, automobile salesmen were notorious for their hard sell tactics.*
b. *I hate to do business with that company. I can't take their hard sell approach.*
c. *He came on to me with a hard sell that really turned me off.*

Hard up

When you have little or no money life can be very hard, giving rise to the expression "hard up," meaning to have less money than is needed. This may also mean that one has not had any sex in some time.

a. *When I was young my family was hard up.*
b. *His brother is always hard up for money because he wastes his salary gambling.*
c. *It is not such a bad thing for students to be hard up for money.*

Hardhead, hardheaded

Describing a person as a "hard head" means they are shrewd and tough. Describing them as "hardheaded" means they are also stubborn and wilful. An additional connotation of this term is that they are also realistic.

a. *It pays to be a hardhead when you are dealing with that guy.*
b. *To be successful, a negotiator has to be hardheaded.*
c. *He is the most hardheaded person I've ever met!*

Have a heart!

Having a heart refers to being kind, generous and helpful, and is, of course, the opposite of being heartless—that is, cruel, selfish.

a. *Come on! Have a heart! Let me borrow your car!*
b. *Can't you have a heart? At least once?*
c. *You want me to have a heart! How about you?*

Have a sharp tongue

Be very critical; make harsh, biting remarks, often when there is no real justification for such comments.

a. *People who have a sharp tongue can be worse than annoying; they can be maddening.*
b. *Well, you knew she had a sharp tongue before you married her!*
c. *Her sharp tongue was her downfall.*

Have a silver tongue

Someone who is a smooth, persuasive talker; often a man who is very clever at talking women into doing things they would not ordinarily do.

a. *Yes, he has a silver tongue, but that's all he has!*
b. *Her boyfriend has a silver tongue, but she likes him anyway.*
c. *That politician is known for his silver tongue.*

Have a way with words

Be a very clever, persuasive talker.

a. *Women are much more likely than men to have a way with words.*
b. *He certainly has a way with words. Maybe he should be a salesman!*
c. *He was elected because he has a way with words; not because he is smart.*

Have a winning hand

This saying is derived from a card game, and refers to having the means or ability to win in whatever is concerned.

a. *As soon as I heard their counter offer, I knew we had a winning hand.*
b. *You can't fool me! I know you have a winning hand!*
c. *I've never seen such luck! He always has a winning hand.*

Have bragging rights

Being the first or best at something, which gives you the "right" to brag about it.

a. *Some people overdo their bragging rights.*
b. *They say they have bragging rights on the smallest music player ever made.*
c. *Having bragging rights is good for business.*

Have one's heart set on

If your "heart is set on something" it means you really want it and won't be satisfied if you don't get it.

a. *I had my heart set on a new car this year, but couldn't afford it.*
b. *She had her heart set on getting married in April but the wedding was delayed.*
c. *My heart was set on taking a cruise last summer, and I finally did.*

Have your cake and eat it too

Being able to enjoy something over and over again; or being able to enjoy something that you do not deserve, or should not be yours to enjoy.

a. *She loved to travel and went into the travel business as a way of having her cake and eating it too.*
b. *If he thinks he can have his cake and eat it too he's crazy!*
c. *Few people get to have their cake and eat it too.*

He puts his pants on one leg at a time

This is a rather curious way of implying that a certain man is no better than anybody else, even though he may be rich or powerful.

a. *Even if he is the president he still puts his pants on one leg at a time.*
b. *No matter how important he acts he still puts his pants on one leg at a time.*
c. *So he's rich! But he still puts his pants on one leg at a time!*

He squats to pee

This is a derogatory remark about a boy or man who acts feminine; an oblique reference to the fact that females customarily squat down to urinate.

a. *That guy squats to pee so you don't have to worry about getting into a fight with him.*

b. *So you think you're tough, do you? I'll bet you squat to pee!*
c. *There is a rumor floating around that the new guy squats to pee.*

He/she is a bloodsucker

This saying derives from bats and other species that live by sucking the blood from other creatures. In colloquial use it refers to someone who takes unfair and often illegal advantage of others.

a. *Forget him! He's a professional bloodsucker!*
b. *Stay away from her! She's a notorious bloodsucker!*
c. *My partner turned out to be a bloodsucker.*

He/she is full of it

When people talk too much about a certain subject, or just about things in general, especially when they are not truly an expert, are often said to be "full of it," which may mean either that they are consumed by the subject, or that they are talking nonsense. A vulgar version of the expression: that's bull-shit.

a. *My wife often makes excuses for me when I carry on about something by smiling and saying "He's full of it!"*
b. *Come on! Knock it off! Everybody knows you're full of it!*
c. *That guy is simple full of it!*

He's on the dance floor but he can't hear the music

This interesting expression refers to being engaged in something, like a major marketing program, in a haphazard, unstructured way and not doing well.

a. *That marketing manager may be on the dance floor but he can't hear the music.*
b. *The new coach said flat out that the team might be on the dance floor but it couldn't hear the music.*
c. *If you are going to get on the dance floor you better be able to hear the music.*

He's smashed

"Smashed" originally referred to something that had been broken into small pieces by some violent action. Now it is also used to mean being completely drunk on alcohol, to the point of collapsing in a heap.

a. *He was smashed before we finished dinner.*
b. *Getting smashed every night is not good for your health!*
c. *He smashed his car against the wall.*

Heads will roll

This expression harks back to the days when beheading was a common way of executing people. Now it refers to people being fired, usually for misconduct or some kind of serious failure.

a. *There was no doubt that heads would roll as a result of the scandal.*
b. *We were told that heads would roll if the new product launch failed.*
c. *The school principal promised that heads would roll because of the misconduct by several teachers.*

Heart is in the right place

Having your "heart in the right place" means you are very kind, sympathetic, well-meaning and otherwise a good person.

a. *Despite his rough manner his heart was in the right place.*
b. *If you want to find out if his heart is in the right place ask him to help you.*
c. *I knew her heart was in the right place from the way she treated children.*

Heart of gold

A person who is kind, generous and has a forgiving nature is often described as having "a heart of gold," inferring a nature that it is rare and precious.

a. *My grandmother had a heart of gold.*

b. *When disaster struck we found out that he had a heart of gold.*
c. *The best way I can describe him is to say that he had a heart of gold.*

Hide one's head in the sand

Ostriches are noted for hiding their heads in the sand when they sense danger. Some people are also said to hide their heads in the sand to avoid seeing, knowing or understanding what is going on.

a. *The problem with some managers is that they hide their heads in the sand and never know what is going on around them.*
b. *If you continue to hide your head in the sand you are going to lose for sure.*
c. *She was so shy she habitually hid her head in the sand.*

High-handed

"High-handed" refers to a type of behavior that is bossy and based on intimidation or force rather than persuasion or willing cooperation.

a. *The new management team took a high-handed approach to transforming the company.*
b. *That kind of high-handed behavior will not get you anywhere!*
c. *The high-handed attitude of the president did not set well with the directors.*

Highway robbery

It used to be common in many countries for robbers to lurk along highways and steal from travelers. This gave rise to the phrase "highway robbery" in reference to sellers charging more for something that it is worth.

a. *Those prices are highway robbery!*
b. *The price that company charges for its services is highway robbery.*
c. *You may think it is fair but I think it is highway robbery.*

His bark is worse than his bite

This saying refers to an individual who has a reputation for being critical and for saying things that are unfriendly, upsetting etc., but in actuality does not behave in that manner.

a. *The supervisor was always threatening to fire anyone who was late but he never did. His bark was worse than his bite.*
b. *His bark is worse than his bite, so forget what he said.*
c. *She knew my bark is worse than my bite, so she just ignored me.*

Hit on

"Hit on" comes from the concept of hitting or attacking, but it now has the thoroughly modern meaning of trying to seduce someone into having sex with you.

a. *That guy hits on every good-looking woman he sees!*
b. *You start hitting on my girlfriend and you're in trouble!*
c. *If you hit on that girl you're liable to get told off.*

Hit the jackpot

Jackpot refers to the stakes in a poker game, a top prize or reward, or to experiencing great success or sudden good fortune. When you "hit the jackpot" it means you win and get the jackpot.

a. *We hit the jackpot at a casino and came home with a lot of money.*
b. *The new product turned out to be a jackpot for the maker.*
c. *If you are always chasing jackpots you may end up being a loser.*

Hit the sauce

In this expression, "sauce" refers to an alcoholic drink, and "hitting the sauce" is a generally derogatory reference to someone drinking to excess.

a. *When his wife divorced him he began to hit the sauce big time.*
b. *Hitting the sauce is not a solution to your problem!*
c. *He lost his job because he just couldn't stop hitting the sauce.*

Hold a losing hand

Have a weak set of cards, or a poor business deal doomed to fail.

a. *The moment he began to speak I knew I had a losing hand.*
b. *Winners never stay in a game when they have a losing hand.*
c. *When he realized he had a losing hand he quits.*

Hold one's breath

There are a number of occasions when people hold their breath for a few seconds, including when they are listening very intently to try to determine what is happening, especially when they are waiting for something very important or critical to happen.

a. *I held my breath while waiting to hear if my name will be called as winner of the prize.*
b. *If you are waiting for me to pay the bill don't hold your breath!*
c. *She held her breath while waiting for his answer.*

Hold one's tongue

"Hold one's tongue" refers to stop talking, to keeping quiet—an obvious extension to actually holding your tongue, which makes it virtually impossible for one to talk.

a. *The teacher told the talking young boy to hold his tongue.*
b. *I could hardly hold my tongue when the policeman started criticizing my driving.*
c. *There are many times when holding your tongue is the best policy.*

Hold out on

"Holding out on" means refusing to divulge some information or refusing to share something tangible with someone, particularly when the other individual has a right to know the information and to a fair share of the thing.

a. *You've been holding out on me!*
b. *The manager made everybody mad by holding out on the company plans.*
c. *He acted like holding out on us was no big deal.*

Hold your horses

"Hold your horses" means to wait, to not be impatient; an indirect reference to the fact that untrained horses often rear up and are hard to hold.

a. *Hold your horses for a moment while I make a phone call.*
b. *Hold your horses! I'm working as fast as I can!*
c. *Can't you hold your horses for a moment?*

Horse around

The expression "horse around" comes from the fact that young horses are very active and playful, and refers to such behavior that is particularly rough and noisy.

a. *Will you two stop horsing around and be still for a moment!*
b. *The teacher told the children to stop horsing around and get ready for class.*
c. *Those guys are in their forties but they still like to horse around.*

Horse of a different color

Something or some idea that is different from what was originally believed, noted, or proposed.

a. *If you can give me a lower price your proposition will be a horse of a different color.*
b. *That politician is just like the rest of them—just a horse of a different color.*
c. *I finally realized I had misjudged him. He was a horse of a different color.*

Horse trade

In earlier times, trading horses, for other horses or other things, was a major activity. To be successful at trading horses you had to be good at judging the value of the horses and whatever was being received in return, which often involved hard-bargaining. Eventually horse trading came to be shrewd and vigorous bargaining.

a. *Our supply manager is a great horse trader.*
b. *It took several hours of horse trading but we finally got the price we wanted.*
c. *In some countries, horse trading is a part of every business deal.*

Hot as a firecracker

Firecrackers appear to be hot because they create red flashes that are spectacular. A product that is selling especially well or an athlete who is performing superbly may be described as hot as a firecracker.

a. *Boy! Last night that batter was as hot as a firecracker!*
b. *I hear your new product is hot as a firecracker.*
c. *You have to be as hot as a firecracker to keep up with him.*

Hot potato

When heated, potatoes hold the heat for a long time, and can cause a painful burn if handled too soon. In this reference a "hot potato" is a situation that is very controversial, is difficult to handle, and is likely to cause harm.

a. *The new contract turned out to be a hot potato.*
b. *The issue of building the nuclear power plant became a real hot potato for the city.*
c. *That lawyer thrives on hot potato issues.*

Hung up on it/her/him

This phrase means to become obsessed with something or somebody, and not being able to think clearly or rationally about the subject.

a. *She is totally hung up on him so you might as well forget your good advice.*
b. *He got hung up on her on the first date.*
c. *I'd get hung up on her too if I had a chance.*

Icing on the cake

Icing on a cake is something extra that makes cake tastes better and more popular as a dessert. It is also used to refer to anything that results in making something more desirable.

a. *Getting an unexpected bonus was just icing on the cake!*
b. *Having his aunt paying for his honeymoon was icing on the cake!*
c. *The great weather on our picnic day was icing on the cake.*

If the shoe fits....!

This phrase is most often used in situations where the truth is obvious but may not have been proven, often said when accusing someone of something.

a. *You claim that you're not guilty, but if the shoe fits...!*
b. *All she had to say to him is "If the shoe fits...!" and he confessed.*
c. *The description fit him like a shoe.*

I'm all ears

"I'm all ears" literally means that you are just two giant ears. Figuratively, it means that you are eager to hear something and are very attentive to what someone is saying.

a. *I understand you have something you want to tell me. Well, go ahead. I'm all ears!*
b. *When she heard whispering behind her desk she became all ears.*
c. *Don't talk about confidential matters in front of him. He's all ears.*

In a heartbeat

The heart beats in a quick, steady rhythm, and is often used in reference to things that happen quickly.

a. *If I were offered a job by that company, I would take it in a heartbeat.*
b. *If that girl asked me to go out I would do it in a heartbeat.*
c. *It was one of those decisions you make in a heartbeat.*

In a nutshell

This very useful expression came from the fact that nutshells are very small but hold the potential of a large tree. It refers to making key points in a very few words.

a. *To give it to you in a nutshell, I'm not going, and that is that!*
b. *The speaker summed up his major points in a nutshell.*
c. *I'm in a hurry. Say what you have to say in a nutshell.*

In black and white

In this case, "black" refers to ink and "white" refers to paper. "In black and white" refers to getting something, like a contract or promise, in writing.

a. *If you ever do any business with him be sure you get every detail in black and white.*
b. *If you don't have it in black and white you don't have a leg to stand on.*
c. *Don't be embarrassed to insist that he put it in black and white.*

In one's hair

Being in or getting "into someone's hair" means to bother or annoying them in some way, either verbally or physically.

a. *If you don't get out of my hair I'm going to pour ice water down your back.*
b. *People don't like her because she is always getting in their hair.*
c. *My sister's small son is always getting in her hair when she is making dinner.*

In one's shoes

"In one's shoes" refers to be in another person's place or position, a situation that is often difficult or dangerous for some reason.

a. *I would hate to be in your shoes when your wife finds out what you have done!*
b. *I would hate to be in his shoes now that he has lost his job.*
c. *Why don't you try being in his shoes for a day! You won't find it easy!*

In the bag

If you put something in a bag you can say with certainty that you have it. "In the bag" is now used in reference to business deals and other things.

a. *It took some serious negotiating but the new contract is in the bag.*
b. *We don't have an agreement yet but I'm sure it's in the bag.*
c. *Don't tell anyone until it's in the bag.*

In the bat of an eye

The eyelids of people and other creatures "bat" (close quickly) every few seconds to keep the eyes moistened, giving rise to the expression "in the bat of an eye" to mean something that happens quickly.

a. *The fire started slowly and then in the bat of an eye it soared to the top of the dry Christmas tree.*

b. *I'd accept that offer in the bat of an eye!*
c. *My bag disappeared from my side in the bat of an eye.*

In the doghouse

Being "in the doghouse" means to be in disfavor, and it denotes punishment for some kind of misbehavior.

a. *If you kids don't stop that you're going to be in the doghouse for the rest of the day!*
b. *John is in the doghouse because he stayed out late last night with his friends.*
c. *If I don't get home soon I will be in the doghouse.*

In the hole

This interesting and very common expression refers to being in debt, to owing more money than you have.

a. *Some people cannot manage their money and are always in the hole.*
b. *If you don't stop spending so recklessly you are going to be in the hole.*
c. *The company spent so much on the marketing program that it went in the hole.*

In the loop

In the loop refers to being kept informed about something that involves a number of people, in the sense that you are an insider and have the same knowledge or involvement as others.

a. *Business executives and politicians often claim that they were not in the loop when something illegal or immoral takes place.*
b. *I was not in the loop so how could I be responsible?*
c. *Well, you're in the loop now, so get on with it!*

In the market

This colloquial expression means that someone is interested in acquiring (buying) something.

a. *My brother-in-law is in the market for a new car.*
b. *That company is in the market for a new CEO.*
c. *Let me know when you are in the market for anything in computers.*

In the works

"In the works" refers to something that is being planned or is already underway.

a. *We have two new products in the works.*
b. *The products we have in the works are scheduled for release this fall.*
c. *We don't have anything in the works at this time.*

Iron out

"Ironing" a piece of clothing with a household iron gets all of the wrinkles out and leaves it smooth, thus the expression "iron out" in the sense of solving disagreements or problems.

a. *It took a while but my girlfriend and I finally got our problems ironed out.*
b. *We have to iron out our differences with that company.*
c. *Let's get the small details ironed out first.*

It takes two to tango

The tango is a dance that requires two partners. The expression has been extended to refer to situations that requires two people, and is usually a negative reference, as in the act of adultery.

a. *He may have started it, but remember, it takes two to tango.*
b. *When my wife told me it takes two to tango I knew I was in for it.*
c. *I knew there was someone else involved when the deal fell through because it takes two to tango.*

It was a breeze

A breeze is generally pleasant and easy to take. Something that is described as a breeze is something easy to do.

a. *The climb up the low mountain was a breeze.*
b. *For some people learning how to use a computer is a breeze.*
c. *It was a breeze for the kids.*

It's as good as done!

This saying means that you will do something quickly, without fail, inferring that it is easy and that you will do it wholeheartedly.

a. *I'll take care of that. It's as good as done!*
b. *I'm your man. It's as good as done.*
c. *If you say it's as good as done you'd better be right. The boss is coming!*

It's on the tip of my tongue

When you are trying to remember something and it seems like you are very close to recalling it, you may say "It's on the tip of my tongue."

a. *My former teacher's name was on the tip of my tongue but I just couldn't get it out!*
b. *It was embarrassing when I had his name on the tip of my tongue, but couldn't remember it.*
c. *All day long I had the feeling it was on the tip of my tongue.*

Itchy palm

The phrase "itchy palm" has come to mean being greedy and having an unrealistic or abnormal desire for money.

a. *The police officer had an itchy palm and started taking money from criminals.*
b. *You can usually tell pretty quickly when someone has an itchy palm.*
c. *His school roommate soon became notorious for having an itchy palm.*

Jack up

A "jack" is a device for raising something up in the air, like a car jack that is used when one has to change a flat tire. "Jack up" refers to raising the car, or, in this case, raising prices.

a. *Just before every holiday that store jacks up its prices.*
b. *The weakest rumor about an oil shortage often results in oil companies jacking up the prices of gasoline.*
c. *Most manufacturers jack up their prices periodically to keep up with inflation.*

Johnny-come-lately

Someone who is late in maturing, in achieving success, or who suddenly becomes popular is often described as a Johnny-come-lately.

a. *That new actor is certainly a Johnny-come-lately.*
b. *Why did that Johnny-come-lately get promoted so quickly?*
c. *Who's the new Johnny-come-lately?*

Jump down one's throat

Becoming very angry and shouting at someone is likened to jumping down their throat, an image that is upsetting to say the least.

a. *His wife jumped down his throat when he came home late for the third day in a row.*
b. *Don't jump down my throat! I didn't do anything!*
c. *My boss became so angry I thought he was going to jump down my throat.*

Jump the gun

Firing a shot from a gun is commonly used to start competitive events. If someone "jumps the gun" they start before they are supposed to.

a. *The marketing department jumped the gun by starting their sales effort before the product was ready.*
b. *The last thing we want to do is jump the gun!*
c. *The race was restarted because one of the runners jumped the gun.*

Just what the doctor ordered

The reputation that doctors have for helping people has been carried over into this expression in reference to anything that is regarded as good or desirable.

a. *The rain after a long drought was just what the doctor ordered.*
b. *The 3-day weekend was just what the doctor ordered.*
c. *When I was transferred to my new job it was just what the doctor ordered.*

Keep a stiff upper lip

The British have often been described as steeling themselves to withstand difficulties by keeping a stiff upper lip—that is, keeping a straight face, not curling their lips.

a. *Don't cry! Try to keep a still upper lip!*
b. *Sometimes keeping a stiff upper lip just doesn't cut it!*
c. *When you hear bad news it's hard to keep a still upper lip.*

Keep on swinging

This expression no doubt came from the world of baseball. It means keep trying; never give up.

a. *It doesn't make any difference how difficult it is, he keeps on swinging.*
b. *If you want to succeed you have to keep on swinging.*
c. *He just keeps on swinging until he connects.*

Keep on trucking

This expression is an extension of the fact that trucks go forward, and is used to mean keep going; don't give up.

a. *I hate this job, but I'll keep on trucking.*
b. *Keep on trucking, or you'll lose your job!*
c. *It's incredible how he keeps on trucking no matter what!*

Keep one's chin up

Keeping one's chin up is a reference to being brave, courageous, not giving up, staying determined to succeed or win in any situation.

a. *We have to keep our chin up if we are going to win the game.*
b. *My brother is trying to keep his chin up even though he has lost his job.*
c. *If you keep your chin up you can succeed.*

Keep one's head

Keeping your head refers to staying calm in a dangerous or stressful situation.

a. *In case of a fire it is very important that you keep your head.*
b. *When the boss started bawling me out I did my best to keep my head.*
c. *Our coach told us to keep our heads and concentrate on the game.*

Keep one's nose to the grindstone

I presume this saying came from the fact that people who used a grindstone to sharpen knives and other instruments had to bend over it, bringing their nose in close proximity to the stone, and keep focused on what they were doing. It is now used to mean working hard or keeping busy for long periods of time

a. *People who keep their nose to the grindstone are the most likely to succeed.*
b. *I told my daughter that if she kept her nose to the grindstone and got good grades in school, I will buy her a car.*
c. *No matter how often he was told to keep his nose to the grindstone he simply couldn't do it.*

Keep someone in the dark

To withhold information from someone, especially information that is secret or may be dangerous in some way is known as keeping the person in the dark.

a. *CEOs accused of illegal actions often say their underlings kept them in the dark.*
b. *Why are you keeping us in the dark about your honeymoon?*
c. *She is keeping everyone in the dark about her college plans.*

Keep under one's hat

This interesting expression refers to keeping something confidential or secret. It dates back to the time when most men and women wore hats.

a. *When I came up with the idea for a new Internet service I knew I had to keep it under my hat.*
b. *She can't keep anything under her hat!*
c. *Let's make sure we keep this under our hat until we file for a patent.*

Keep your nose out of my business!

Since the nose protrudes out from the face, it is used in the sense of "sticking it" into the affairs of others.

a. *If you don't keep your nose out of my business you'll be sorry!*
b. *She's always sticking her nose into other people's business.*
c. *I will not stick my nose into other people's business.*

Keep your pants on!

I'm not sure how this expression came about, but it means be patient.

a. *Rome wasn't built in a day. Keep your pants on!*
b. *You would be a lot better off if you learned how to keep your pants on.*
c. *All I said was keep your pants on, but she got mad anyway!*

Keep your shirt on!

Taking your shirt off used to be a sign that you were getting ready to engage in some kind of activity that was especially demanding or dirty, and was a demonstration of how anxious you were to get started. Telling someone to keep their shirt on means "be patient," "don't get excited."

a. *We've got plenty of time. Keep your shirt on!*
b. *Tell him to keep his shirt on. I'll be there in a few minutes.*
c. *Okay! I'll keep my shirt on, but hurry!*

Kick back and relax

Kick back originally referred to kicking a ball back. Now it also means relaxing and enjoying yourself.

a. *After a hard day's work I like to kick back and relax, and watch a science fiction movie.*
b. *She likes to go to a spa, kick back and relax for a whole weekend.*
c. *Let's just kick back and relax tonight!*

Kick up one's heels

This is another common expression that probably came from the animal world, particularly young animals that kick up their heels in play. It means to have a good time; to celebrate.

a. *Let's go out tonight and kick up our heels!*
b. *Go ahead and kick up your heels, but remember we have to work tomorrow!*
c. *Rock stars and sports figures are notorious for kicking up their heels.*

Kill the goose that lays the golden eggs

This interesting expression refers to doing something that kills or spoils a very good deal of some kind; especially one that is very profitable.

a. *When they let the patent run out it killed the goose that laid the golden eggs.*
b. *Losing the government contract killed the goose that laid the golden eggs.*
c. *If you continue on that approach you will kill the goose that lays the golden eggs.*

Kiss it/them goodbye

Said when something disappears or becomes unavailable, and there is no hope of it being returned.

a. *If you leave your bags unattended in that airport you might as well kiss them goodbye.*
b. *I might as well kiss my dreams goodbye.*
c. *If you've paid in advance for that thing you might as well kiss your money goodbye.*

Knock a person off their feet

The colloquial meaning of this expression is to surprise or shock someone to the point that they are figuratively knocked off their feet.

a. *When she entered the room in her low-cut gown I was knocked off my feet.*
b. *When the company announced that it was closing down the plant it knocked the employees off their feet.*
c. *His speech was so eloquent I was knocked off my feet.*

Land on one's feet

This expression is an extension of the ability of cats to land on their feet even when dropped upside down. It means to come out of a bad situation without suffering any damage or loss.

a. *When the company declared bankruptcy only the top executives landed on their feet.*
b. *He was very good at landing on his feet, regardless of the situation.*
c. *If we don't land on our feet this time we can always start over.*

Laughing stock

In the early years of American history, some people convicted of minor crimes had their heads and hands secured between planks of wood attached to the ground in a public area, resulting in people laughing at them.

a. *If you wear that silly hat it will make you the laughing stock of the party!*
b. *When I tried to sing I immediately became a laughing stock.*
c. *Becoming a laughing stock can ruin your chances of being promoted.*

Lay down the law

"Laying down the law" refers to telling someone precisely what is expected of them; what they can do and what they can't do; the rules they are expected to follow.

a. *The coach laid down the law to the new players.*
b. *My girlfriend laid down the law to me.*
c. *The principal laid down the law to the new students.*

Lay out

The expression "lay out" has been extended to mean to pay money or to spend money.

a. *I had to lay out a lot of cash for the new software.*
b. *If you are not willing to lay out a big sum of money you can't buy that car.*
c. *The company was prepared to lay out a huge sum to buy its competitor.*

Leave a bad taste in one's mouth

"Leave a bad taste in your mouth" refers to some incident, some word or some action, that disturbs you, makes you angry, makes a bad impression on you, and is unpleasant in some way.

a. *His comment about my girlfriend left a bad taste in my mouth.*
b. *My experience with the rude sales clerk left a bad taste in my mouth.*
c. *The way that the company treated the workers left a bad taste in their mouths.*

Leave no stone unturned

Never stop until you have exhausted every avenue, every possible approach to finding an answer or achieving some other result.

a. *The police left no stone unturned in searching for the kidnapped child.*
b. *If we want the marketing plan to succeed we can't leave a stone unturned.*
c. *She left no stone unturned in questioning me.*

Let it go

Stop worrying about it; stop talking about it; forget it.

a. *If you don't let it go, I'm going to kick your butt!*
b. *I hate arguing with her because she never lets anything go.*
c. *I know it was insulting but just let it go!*

Let it ride

This phrase is often used in gambling when a player decides to keep a bet on the table. It also applies to other situations when the choice is to let it stay the same; to make no changes.

a. *I'm satisfied with our contract. Let's let it ride.*
b. *When I asked about paying him back he said let it ride.*
c. *I'm too busy to think about it now so just let it ride.*

Let one's hair down

Having one's "hair up" suggests a formal situation and formal behavior, so "letting one's hair down" is just the opposite—being relaxed and informal in your behavior.

a. *When the boss left we let our hair down and had a good time.*
b. *If you don't let your hair down occasionally you miss a lot of fun.*
c. *As soon as the drinking started, everybody let their hair down.*

Let sleeping dogs lie

This common expression means don't do anything that might cause some kind of trouble or result in extra work.

a. *Keep quiet about that! Let sleeping dogs lie!*
b. *If you don't let sleeping dogs lie you're sure to get into some kind of trouble.*
c. *After giving it careful thought I decided to let sleeping dogs lie.*

Let the cat out of the bag

In earlier times, people used to kill newly born kittens (to keep the cat population down) by putting them into a gunny sack, adding some rocks, tying the top, and tossing the bag into a creek or river. Letting the cat out of the bag has come to mean revealing secrets.

a. *My daughter let the cat out of the bag, so I knew the family was planning a birthday party for me.*
b. *We were warned not to let the cat out of the bag.*
c. *The boss really got mad when someone let the cat out of the bag about our new product.*

Let the chips fall where they may

When chopping wood, there is no way to control where the chips are going to fall. This phrase came into use in reference to doing something regardless of what the repercussions or outcome might be.

a. *I decided to let the chips fall where they may, and told my boss I was going to quit if he didn't give me a raise.*
b. *I don't care about that. Let the chips fall where they may.*
c. *He says whatever comes to his mind and let the chips fall where they may.*

Let the grass grow under your feet

People who are lazy and inactive may be described as letting grass grow under their feet.

a. *Successful people are generally those who never let grass grow under their feet.*
b. *He spent his life letting the grass grow under his feet, and was as happy as a lark.*
c. *Come on! Get moving! Stop letting the grass grow under your feet!*

Lift a finger

"Lift a finger" refers to doing something, helping someone, and usually has a negative connotation.

a. *He was the kind of person who would never lift a finger to help anyone.*
b. *If everybody would lift a finger once in a while to help others it would be wonderful.*
c. *I will not lift a finger to help you until you mend your ways!*

Light on his/her feet

This was originally a phrase used to describe people who were good dancers and looked like they were virtually floating around the dance floor. Now it is used in reference to people, especially business people, who are quick thinkers and fast decisions makers.

a. *The new CEO is really light on his feet.*
b. *You have to be light on your feet to keep up with her.*
c. *That company only hires people who are light on their feet.*

Like a bat out of hell

In the late evenings bats fly out of their caves with great speed, giving rise to the saying "like a bat out of hell." It means moving or doing something very fast.

a. *This morning the boss came into the office like a bat out of hell.*
b. *He drives like a bat out of hell.*
c. *He left here like a bat out of hell. I don't know why he was in such a hurry.*

Like a breath of fresh air

A sudden breeze or gust of fresh air can be very invigorating and invoke a pleasant feeling. So can some event or some news.

a. *Seeing her again was like a breath of fresh air!*
b. *This work is killing me. I need a breath of fresh air.*
c. *John just went out for a breath of fresh air.*

Like a bump on a log

A bump on a log may spoil its use in building or making furniture, etc., so logs with bumps may be passed over. This phrase refers to something that is very conspicuous, out of place, undesirable, useless, etc.

a. *Don't sit there like a bump on a log! Get out on the dance floor!*
b. *Those girls act like bumps on a log because they are bashful.*
c. *I feel like a bump on a log!*

Like a duck takes to water

Something that happens easily, naturally, the way ducks head for water the moment they spot it.

a. *Young children take to computers the way ducks take to water.*
b. *The visitor took to Japanese food like a duck takes to water.*
c. *Just try it! I'm sure you will take to it like ducks take to water.*

Like a herd of elephants

When a herd of elephants move, they can be destructive, walking over or through anything that gets in their way. They can also be noisy.

a. *When the bell rang the students emerged from the building like a herd of elephants.*
b. *The shoppers rushed into the store like a herd of elephants.*
c. *Remember! Be calm; be relaxed; not like a herd of elephants.*

Like a pit bull

A pit bull is a dog that is especially powerful, tends to be very aggressive, and once it starts something it will not give up until it succeeds or is stopped by some greater force—a description that is often applied to people who demonstrate similar traits.

a. *Some men are so aggressive that they come on like pit bulls.*
b. *If you are going to succeed in this business you have to behave like a pit bull.*
c. *He came on like a pit bull so she dumped him after the first date.*

Like hell you will!

When said to someone, this expression means that under no circumstances are you going to allow them to do something.

a. *You say you're going to take my girlfriend out? Like hell you will!*
b. *Beat me at bowling! Like hell you will!*
c. *When she said she was going to drop him, he said "Like hell you will!"*

Like putty in his hands

Before it hardens, putty is soft and pliable and can be shaped easily. Saying that someone is putty in your hands infers that you can control them easily.

a. *The girl was so young and naïve she was like putty in his hands.*
b. *The crowd was putty in the hands of the speaker.*
c. *Their team is second-rate. They will be putty in our hands.*

Like shooting fish in a barrel

Obviously, if you put fish in a barrel they would be easy to shoot. Thus anything that is easy to do can be referred to as like shooting fish in a barrel.

a. *The salesman said that getting customers to sign up for the new insurance was like shooting fish in a barrel.*
b. *Mike says that picking up girls is like shooting fish in a barrel.*
c. *This is too easy! It's like shooting fish in a barrel!*

Like two peas in a pod

Two things that are perfectly identical, especially identical twins, are often said to be like two peas in a pod. The phrase is also used in other more general references.

a. *When the detective compared the two bullets, he said they were like two peas in a pod.*
b. *My brother and my uncle look like two peas in a pod.*
c. *The five kittens look like two peas in a pod.*

Like water off a duck's back

"Like water off a duck's back" refers to something that has little or no effect, like criticism that is ignored.

a. *He is so thick-skinned that criticism runs off him like water off a duck's back.*

b. *The operation went as smoothly as water off a duck's back.*
c. *Success came to him as easily as water off a duck's back.*

Lip service

This interesting expression refers to supporting something verbally, by words, but not by actions, and is therefore worth very little or nothing.

a. *All I ever get from that company is lip service.*
b. *Most politicians are experts at lip service.*
c. *If lip service is all I am going to get, then forget it!*

Live and let live

This expression refers to a policy or philosophy of being very tolerant toward other ideas, other people, as well as animals, with a minimum of regulation and restrictions.

a. *One of the principles of democracy is live and let live.*
b. *His only real philosophy is live and let live.*
c. *People who go by the live and let live rule are usually happy.*

Live it up

A very popular expression that means to really enjoy one's self; to dispense with restraints and enjoy something enthusiastically.

a. *Let's go out and live it up tonight!*
b. *From the way you look you must have really lived it up last night!*
c. *I like to live it up, but I don't like to go too far!*

Live the life of Riley

Riley was presumably a rich man who lived an envious lifestyle, enjoying all of the amenities that his wealth could buy.

a. *As soon as the couple won the lottery they begin to live the life of Riley.*
b. *They live the life of Riley because their rich relatives are generous!*
c. *He's still dreaming about living the life of Riley.*

Living high on the hog

It may be that the higher on the body of a hog, the tastier the meat. In any event, the "top" of a hog is usually cleaner and more attractive than the bottom, so some wit came up with the idea of describing living in a luxurious manner as living high on a hog.

a. *Since that couple won the lottery, they have been living high on the hog.*
b. *If I ever become rich I'm going to live high on the hog.*
c. *The politician became notorious for living high on the hog.*

Living in La La land

This is an expression that is used to describe someone whose lifestyle is far out, unrealistic, as in a fairyland.

a. *Newly rich rock stars and other entertainers often end up in La La land, spaced out on drugs and their fame.*
b. *Get real! Stop acting like you are in La La land!*
c. *The employees of some start-up companies act like they are in La La land.*

Loaded

In addition to is original meaning (that something has been loaded on a truck, for example) this term is also used to mean that a person is drunk as well as that he or she has lots of money—in other words, really well off if not rich.

a. *My uncle was very successful in business and is now loaded.*
b. *That guy gets loaded (drunk) every night.*
c. *You have to be loaded to join that club.*

Look before you leap

Leaping into anything, especially something like a muddy river, before checking it out can be a dangerous thing.

a. *I warned him to look before he leap but he got married anyway.*

b. *Many business people fail to look before they leap into new markets.*
c. *You should also look before you leap into anything.*

Look down one's nose

It seems that in the past upper class people would keep their heads high and "look down their noses" at common people. This apparently resulted in the expression coming to mean regarding something or someone as low-class or worthless, and be scornful of them.

a. *My neighbors look down their noses at my old pickup truck, but I love it.*
b. *Some children are taught to look down their noses at people who work with their hands.*
c. *Looking down your nose at anybody or anything is a narrow minded thing to do.*

Look like a cat that swallowed a canary

In the past people used to keep canaries in cages, and their cats would sometimes manage to get hold of the canaries and eat them, no doubt feeling smug and satisfied afterward. This resulted in the expression "looking like a cat that swallowed a canary" coming to mean a smug or self-satisfied look on a person's face.

a. *You look like a cat that swallowed a canary. What happened?*
b. *When I walked into the room I must have looked like a cat that had just swallowed a canary.*
c. *She definitely looks like a cat that swallowed a canary. I wonder what she has been up to!*

Lose heart

To "lose heart" refers to becoming discouraged for some reason, losing hope for survival or success or for any desirable thing.

a. *I began to lose heart after realizing I was not going to be hired by that company.*
b. *He lost heart when his wife died, and was never the same again.*
c. *Don't lose heart if you fail the exam for your driver's license. Study harder and try again!*

Lose one's shirt

Losing one's shirt does not mean you lost your shirt. It means you lost a lot of money; in some cases all of the money you had.

a. *I got involved in a business deal that resulted in me losing my shirt.*
b. *He lost his shirt at a casino in Las Vegas.*
c. *Be careful about going into business with him. You could lose your shirt!*

Losing her/his grip

If you are holding onto something while dangling from a height, you may be in serious trouble if you lose your grip. Now, people who lose control of their emotions, or become unable to accomplish tasks at their usual level of competence are said to be losing their grip.

a. *That CEO is definitely losing his grip.*
b. *Get hold of yourself! You're losing your grip!*
c. *As soon as he started talking I knew he had lost his grip on the job.*

Mad as a hornet

Hornets are very protective of their nests and get mad quickly when someone or something disturbs them. People who are very angry and in a fighting mood are often said to be as mad as a hornet.

a. *I was as mad as a hornet when I saw that someone had scratched my new car.*
b. *She got as mad as a hornet when he criticized her singing.*
c. *If you're the type who get as mad as a hornet you'd better learn how to keep a rein on your feelings.*

Made for each other

Said of things or people that are perfectly compatible, perfectly suited, perfectly matched.

a. *As soon as I met her I knew we were made for each other.*
b. *That car and I were made for each other!*
c. *I thought we were made for each other but, boy, was I wrong!*

Make a go of it

If you "make a go of it" it means you have achieved some degree of success.

a. *The start-up company simply could not make a go of it because it had no cash.*
b. *It is a wonderful thing to see young entrepreneurs make a go of it.*
c. *The two students were absolutely sure they could make a go of it so they quit school when they were in their third year.*

Make a killing

This old expression, which goes back to the days when hunting animals for food was common, now means to make a large amount of money; usually in a very short period of time.

a. *My brother made a killing when he worked overseas in the oil industry.*

b. *He is always trying to make a killing with some kind of deal.*
c. *Many people have made a killing on the Internet.*

Make a mountain out of a molehill

Turn something very small into something very big; like inflating a minor complaint or problem into something that looks or sounds very serious.

a. *That woman is a genius at making a mountain out of a molehill!*
b. *That politician is famous for making mountains out of molehills.*
c. *Come on! It was nothing! You're making a mountain out of a molehill!*

Make ends meet

Making ends meet originally referred to something like connecting roads, or tunnels, etc. Now it refers to having enough money to pay bills or expenses.

a. *At the end of the month he never has enough money to make ends meet.*
b. *If we can make ends meet this month we should be in good shape.*
c. *I was shocked when I discovered that I didn't have enough money to make ends meet.*

Make every shot count

In basketball, golf and shooting contests, making every shot count is common sense. The expression is also used in other instances.

a. *If you are going to tangle with that guy you'd better make every shot count!*
b. *I have to make every shot count if I'm going to win.*
c. *You had better make every shot count if you want to keep up with me.*

Make eyes at

"Making eyes at" someone means to flirt with them by winking and giving them coquettish looks to attract their attention and let them know you are interested in them.

a. *In Mexico it is very common for boys to stand on street corners and make eyes at passing girls.*
b. *I can't help it. When I see a pretty girl I just have to make eyes at her.*
c. *My efforts to meet the girl by making eyes at her failed completely. She turned up her nose and looked away.*

Make hay while the sun shines

This is an old saying that relates to cutting grass and other plants to make fodder for livestock feed, something that is best done when the sun is shining and the grass is dry. Now it also refers to pursuing any goal when the possibility of success is the greatest.

a. *If you are going to succeed in business you had better make hay while the sun shines.*
b. *He has a great knack for making hay while the sun shines.*
c. *My wife is out of town so I am going to make hay while the sun shines!*

Make heads or tails

If you cannot understand a problem or puzzle, or something that is said or that you are looking at, it is common to say that you can't "make heads or tails" of it.

a. *The design was so complex I couldn't make heads or tails of it.*
b. *I listened very carefully to his lecture but I couldn't make heads or tails of the point he was trying to make.*
c. *See if you can make heads or tails of this. I don't get it at all.*

Make headway

This expression makes use of the fact that you more or less lead with your head when you are moving forward, especially when you are facing strong winds—known as head winds—or some other obstacle. Make headway means to make progress.

a. *We worked on the problem for several hours but made very little headway.*

b. *The only way we can make headway is to work together.*
c. *Every once in a while the boss stopped by to check on our headway.*

Make light of it

Downplay something; not give credibility to it, especially when it is something that might be damaging or upsetting if it is taken seriously.

a. *Every time I brought up the subject of more money, my boss made light of it.*
b. *This is a serious matter and you shouldn't make light of it.*
c. *Forget him! He makes light of everything!*

Make my day

This term is from an old Clint Eastwood movie, and refers to some action that becomes the highlight of the day.

a. *Meeting you by accident made my day!*
b. *Having Sunday brunch with my brothers made my day.*
c. *Seeing her again made my day.*

Make one's mouth water

Something edible that smells good may make your mouth salivate with anticipation, resulting in this popular expression being used in a variety of situations.

a. *The smell of the freshly baked bread made my mouth water.*
b. *When he saw the new car in the showroom it made his mouth water.*
c. *Just the thought of sukiyaki is enough to make my mouth water.*

Make the cut

In competitive situations where many contestants are involved, there is often an elimination process to reduce the number of individuals. Those with the lowest scores or qualifications are "cut" from the list until a prescribed number is reached. Those who "make the cut" remain in contention.

a. *I applied for a grant but didn't make the cut.*
b. *He wanted to play football but he didn't make the cut.*
c. *You have to be in the upper ten percent of your class to make the cut.*

Mark my words

This is another way of saying something like "remember what I said," when assuring someone that something is going to happen just the way you described or predicted.

a. *Mark my words. He will come to a bad end if he doesn't change his ways.*
b. *You'll see! Just mark my words!*
c. *The last time you told me to mark your words you were wrong!*

Match made in heaven

When two things, especially a man and a woman, are perfectly matched, they are often described as a match made in heaven, one that is divinely ordained.

a. *The merger of those two companies was a match made in heaven.*
b. *We thought it would be a match made in heaven, but it blew up in our face.*
c. *Hoping for a match made in heaven can be a waste of time.*

Meat and potatoes man

Meat and potatoes have been staples of the American working man's diet for generations. The saying now refers to someone who has very simple tastes in food and other things.

a. *I'm a meat and potatoes man so don't take me to a fancy restaurant!*
b. *When it comes to sex he is a meat and potatoes man.*
b. *I would rather have a simple meat and potatoes job.*

Minding your p's and q's

In old England ale was served at local taverns in a "tankard" and drinkers were charged by the angle of their elbows: half-way up and you were charged for a pint. If your elbow went all the way up it meant you drank a quart. Since a quart of ale costs more than the pint, you were warned to "mind your p's & q's." Now the expression is usually written as minding your p's and q's, and refers to minding your manners, or behaving in an accepted manner.

a. *It is especially important to mind your p's and q's when you are in a foreign country.*
b. *The teacher reminded the students to mind their p's and q's.*
c. *The new employees were very careful about minding their p's and q's.*

Mixed bag of tricks

Trying a variety of tactics is often described as a mixed bag of tricks.

a. *That coach is noted for using a mixed bag of tricks to win.*
b. *This isn't a good plan! It looks more like a mixed bag of tricks!*
c. *Some salesmen are clever at using a mixed bag of tricks to make a sale.*

Money doesn't grow on trees

This old adage refers to the well-known fact that most people have to work for the money they get.

a. *When his wife goes shopping he always reminds her that money doesn't grow on trees!*
b. *Some young people act like money grows on trees!*
c. *When you watch people shopping it's hard to believe that money doesn't grow on trees!*

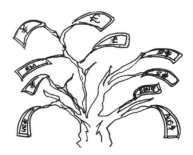

Money talks

As is well know, money can be very persuasive in getting people to do things, and in this sense it "talks."

a. *At first he said he would never take the job, but money talks!*
b. *He was elected simply because money talks!*
c. *If you want me to help you remember that money talks!*

Money to burn

If someone has more money than they need, or will ever spend, it is said that they have "money to burn."

a. *My aunt has money to burn and is always traveling somewhere.*
b. *Some people act like they have money to burn when they are just big spenders putting on an act.*
c. *If I had money to burn I would buy a huge yacht and live on it.*

Monkey business

Monkeys, like people, are known for being curious and getting into trouble because they look into, check out, and mess around with anything new that they come across. This practice resulted in the phrase "monkey business," referring to some kind of mischievous, unethical or bad behavior.

a. *You'd better stop that monkey business and get serious!*
b. *I could tell from the look on his face that he had been up to some kind of monkey business.*
c. *What kind of monkey business have you been up to lately?*

Monkey see monkey do

It is universally recognized that monkeys as well as people tend to imitate the behavior they see.

a. *Don't do that in front of children. Remember, monkey see monkey do!*
b. *It was a classic case of monkey see monkey do.*
c. *When it comes to touching wet paint it's monkey see monkey do!*

More bang for the buck

In this expression "bang" has the meaning of value, and refers to getting more value for the money you spend. "Buck" is an old word meaning one dollar.

a. *We got more bang for our buck when we advertised on the Internet.*
b. *If you want to get more bang for your buck don't buy the cheapest thing you can find.*
c. *I wanted more bang for my buck so I hired a professional ad man.*

My eyes were bigger than my stomach

It is fairly common for people to put more food on their plate than they can eat, especially when at a buffet. When this happens, a common excuse is for them to say that their eyes are bigger than their stomachs.

a. *My eyes were bigger than my stomach, so no dessert for me, thank you!*
b. *I never learn! My eyes are always bigger than my stomach!*
c. *He knows his eyes are bigger than his stomach, but that doesn't stop him!*

My/his/her goose was cooked

This saying refers to a situation in which the person concerned has no chance of success, no possibility of coming out on top, no chance of avoiding something.

a. *As soon as I heard the news I knew my goose was cooked.*
b. *When my girlfriend began accusing me I knew my goose was cooked.*
c. *His goose was cooked the moment he opened his mouth.*

Nail down

The original meaning of "nail down" is to fasten a board or some other piece of material to something else with the use of metal nails. The term has since come to mean to make certain of something, to finally finish something, to get an agreement.

a. *It took all day but we finally nailed down an agreement.*
b. *We have to nail this down before we leave.*
c. *All our attempts to nail down a contract failed.*

Nest egg

Birds and other fowls lay their eggs in nests and the eggs are essential for the survival of their species, giving rise to the term "nest egg," meaning money that one has saved up for some special purpose.

a. *She worked part-time after school and saved up a big nest egg.*
b. *I was never able to build up a nest egg when I was a student.*
c. *Having a sizeable nest egg gave him a sense of security.*

Never judge a book by its cover

Just as the cover of a book does not necessarily reflect its content, the appearance of a person may not reveal his or her true character or ability, thus the use of this saying when talking about people.

a. *Boy, was I wrong about her! I should have remembered that you never judge a book by its cover!*
b. *Well, I warned you about judging a book by its cover.*
c. *It is difficult to avoid judging a book by its cover, especially with people like that!.*

Never look a gift horse in the mouth

In earlier times one of the best ways of determining the health of a horse was to open its mouth and look at its teeth. This led to the expression "never look a gift horse in the mouth," meaning that you shouldn't complain about something you receive as a gift.

a. *You shouldn't look a gift horse in the mouth! It's selfish and rude!*

b. *I don't like to give her gifts because she always looks a gift horse in the mouth.*

c. *If you're going to look a gift horse in the mouth I'll take it back!*

No matter which way you slice it

This expression means that no matter what you do, the outcome is not going to change.

a. *No matter which way you slice it, your proposition is not acceptable.*

b. *No matter which way I slice it she wouldn't accept my excuse.*

c. *No matter how you slice it he is not going to agree with you.*

No skin off one's nose

The expression "no skin off my nose" has come to mean something that doesn't concern me, doesn't bother me and has nothing to do with me.

a. *It's no skin off my nose if I don't get invited to the party.*

b. *Suit yourself! It's no skin off my nose!*

c. *I don't care what he said. It's no skin off my nose.*

Nose around

To "nose around" means to casually look for something, a saying that probably derived from the habit of dogs to "lead with their noses" and sniff everything they come near.

a. *The man I saw nosing around the hotel lobby turned out to be a detective.*
b. *What are you nosing around here for?*
c. *If you continue nosing around like that you could get into trouble.*

Not fit to tie her/his shoes

Tying one's shoes does not require a high order of skill or intelligence, and if someone is not qualified to do that simple chore he or she must really be a loser.

a. *That guy is not fit to tie her shoes!*
b. *Just one look at him and you know he isn't fit to tie her shoes!*
c. *I wouldn't let that guy tie my shoes!*

Not my cup of tea

For many people drinking a cup of hot tea is one of the most pleasant things in life. This gave rise to the expression "not my cup of tea," meaning something that doesn't appeal to you; that you don't like.

a. *Going to the opera is not my cup of tea.*
b. *It turned out that she wasn't my cup of tea.*
c. *I quickly became aware that the new job was not my cup of tea.*

Number cruncher

This is a slang term for an accountant or anyone who works with numbers. It may be negative or positive, depending on how it is used.

a. *Today you have to be, or have, a good number cruncher to succeed in business.*
b. *He really bugs his employees because he looks at everything as a number cruncher.*
c. *The company brought in an outside number cruncher to help them.*

Nutty as a fruitcake

Nuts are one of the most important ingredients in fruitcakes. "Nuts" is also a colloquial way of saying "crazy," as in "you're nuts!" So calling someone "nutty as a fruitcake" is to call them crazy. But, the expression is rather light-hearted and is commonly used among friends in a casual way.

a. *She had one drink and started acting as nutty as a fruitcake.*
b. *If you keep that up people are going to think you're as nutty as a fruitcake.*
c. *He put on an act of being as nutty as a fruitcake.*

Off-color

In this expression something that is "off-color" is considered in bad taste, rude or "dirty."

a. *When he told an off-color joke at the party it made his wife very angry.*
b. *The whole tone of the conversation in the men's locker room was off-color.*
c. *The advertisement was so off-color it was cancelled.*

Off one's chest

Something pressing on your chest can be very uncomfortable or painful. This expression refers to something that a person has on their mind that is bothering them and the only way to relieve the discomfort or pain is to "get it off their chest."

a. *If it bothers you that much, tell me and get it off your chest.*
b. *I have been wanting to get something off my chest for a long time.*
c. *The moment he got it off his chest he felt a great sense of relief.*

Off the record

Something that is "off the record" is not official, not to be published or not to be revealed in any way.

a. *The official said he would answer questions only if his replies were off the record.*
b. *I told my boss off the record that I had received a big order but wanted to keep it confidential for a while.*
c. *Somehow, everything he said off the record became public knowledge.*

Off the top of one's head

This expression means to say something quickly, without thinking deeply or seriously about the subject. The expression infers that the comment is not based on careful consideration, and may therefore not be the final answer.

a. *Off the top of my head I would say there are about 125 million people in Japan.*
b. *The professor didn't like his students to respond off the tops of their heads.*
c. *All I can do now is give you an answer off the top of my head.*

On a shoestring

A shoestring is, of course, a small and relatively unimpressive thing. This concept has been expanded to "on a shoestring," which refers to making some kind of investment with a very small amount of money.

a. *He started his business on a shoestring but now it is very successful.*
b. *It is amazing how many big, famous companies were started on a shoestring.*
c. *Even if we have to start on a shoestring, let's try it.*

On one's shoulders

In this expression, having something on one's shoulders means to be responsible for it.

a. *I don't want that burden on my shoulders; so don't tell me about it.*
b. *Although he wasn't responsible the failure of the project was put on his shoulders.*
c. *I have enough on my shoulders now. I don't want any more responsibility.*

On one's toes

Being "on your toes" suggests that you are ready to begin a race or to face any danger that might be near, and in this expression it means to be alert, paying attention and ready to act.

a. *The speaker kept the audience on their toes by asking many interesting questions.*
b. *You have to be on your toes to keep up with that person.*
c. *He was on his toes the instant the alarm sounded.*

On the block

In earlier years when craftsmen and others put their merchandise up for sale it was often displayed on some kind of wooden block. Nowadays, when something is for sale it is said to be on the block.

a. *When the employees heard that the company was on the block they became very excited.*
b. *That company was on the block for only a few hours before it was snapped up.*
c. *We put the company on the block to see if anyone is interested in buying it.*

On the cuff/Off the cuff

These sayings somehow evolved from the cuff that is at the bottom of a sleeve. On the cuff means without immediately payment, or on credit. Off the cuff means to do something without prior planning or preparation, as in giving a speech.

a. *He made an eloquent speech off the cuff for over an hour!*
b. *If you will sell this to me on the cuff I'll take buy it.*
c. *Giving an off-the-cuff lecture on a highly technical subject was easy for him.*

On the house

"On the house" is an interesting way of saying that the owner of a business absorbs the cost of something—a meal at a restaurant, a tab at a bar, etc.—making it free to the customer.

a. *We went to a restaurant owned by one of my friends and our whole bill was on the house.*
b. *Some restaurants run specials during which everything is on the house.*
c. *I feel like a big shot when I go to a place and everything is on the house.*

On top of the world

A figurative way of saying that someone is doing or feeling great; that things couldn't be better.

a. *When I got the news, I was on top of the world!*
b. *You act like you're on top of the world. What's up?*
c. *Getting a raise put me on top of the world.*

One for the road

"One for the road" generally refers to having a final drink before leaving a place; a custom that became deeply embedded in some cultures as a sign of hospitality, goodwill, manliness and a carefree attitude.

a. *It is still common for some people to insist that you have one for the road before your leave a bar, club or party.*
b. *It is sometimes difficult to resist aggressive hosts who keep insisting that you have one for the road.*
c. *My response is always that one for the road is the last thing I need.*

One good turn deserves another

This very common saying is self-explanatory. If someone does you a good turn (a favor) it is only fair that you do them a favor on some other occasion.

a. *If you believe in and practice the concept of one good turn deserves another your life will be a lot better.*
b. *My whole life has been based on the idea that one good turn deserves another.*
c. *Our business is based on the idea that one good turn deserves another.*

One up on someone

This old expression means to get "one up on someone" by coming up with a better joke, a wittier remark, a better product, or something that puts him ahead or out in front, often just for "bragging rights."

a. *When I won the bowling game my friend admitted that I was one up on him.*
b. *He got a promotion before I did so he was one up on me.*
c. *The new electronic device put us one up on everyone else in the industry.*

One's number is up

The idea of one's "number is up" originally referred to it being your turn if you were waiting in some kind of line in which people were numbered. Now the saying is most often used in reference to something bad happening.

a. *When my boss called me in I knew my number was up.*
c. *When I heard that he had come down with cancer I knew his number was up.*
b. *The hostage was afraid that his number was up.*

One's opposite number

This expression refers to someone who has the same position as oneself in another company or organization, a key element in business, diplomatic and political relationships.

a. *The engineer called his opposite number in Japan when a technical problem came up.*
b. *If you can't reach your opposite number try his or her assistant.*
c. *Establishing a personal relationship with your opposite number is a prerequisite of diplomacy.*

Open book

Someone who is easy to figure out, who is not hiding anything or not good at hiding things, is commonly compared to an open book that can be read.

a. *My wife can read me as if I were an open book!*
b. *Women can read most men like open books.*
c. *His face is an open book.*

Out like a light

This refers to someone who falls asleep the moment they go to bed, to someone who suddenly faints or passes out from over-drinking, and to someone who is hit hard enough to be rendered unconscious.

a. *I was so exhausted that the moment I laid down I was out like a light.*
b. *After just three drinks he was out like a light.*
c. *On the very first punch the boxer was out like a light.*

Out of my/your league

"Your league" refers to the level of your skill or character, and when used infers that you have taken on more than you can handle.

a. *It would be a great job but it is definitely out of your league!*
b. *I'm not going to bowl with you! You're way out of my league!*
c. *She dropped me as a dancing partner when she found out I wasn't in her social league.*

Out of the blue

Originally, "out of the blue" referred to the depths of the blue sky or the blue ocean. In this context it means somebody or something that shows up or occurs without any warning, and is usually a surprise.

a. *Right out of the blue my friend decided to quit his job and move to Paris.*
b. *The announcement of the closure of the plant was out of the blue.*
c. *His out of the blue appearance shocked everyone.*

Out of the frying pan into the fire

Escaping or leaving one dangerous or bad situation only to end up in another situation that is equally bad or dangerous is often characterized as going from a frying pan into a fire—meaning that you are as bad off as you were before.

a. *The day he reported to the new department he knew he had just got out of the frying pan into the fire.*
b. *I was so disappointed when I realized I had just changed from a frying pan to a fire.*
c. *He complained that his second marriage had been like jumping out of the frying pan into the fire.*

Over one's head

A ball that is thrown high over your head obviously cannot be caught. This gave birth to the expression "over one's head," meaning that it is beyond one's ability to understand.

a. *His whole lecture was over my head.*
b. *The engineer's explanation went right over my head.*
c. *If I'm talking over your head, let me know.*

Pain in the neck

A person who is bothersome, obnoxious and otherwise very unpleasant to be around is often described as "a pain in the neck."

a. *You can really be a pain in the neck when you want to!*
b. *Stop being a pain in the neck and do something useful!*
c. *She was such a pain in the neck that her boyfriend finally ditched her.*

Paint oneself into a corner

People have been known to end up in a corner of a room when painting a floor, thus having to walk on wet paint to get out of the room. In other words, "painting yourself into a corner" is not a smart thing to do. The expression is used in reference to someone getting into an awkward or bad situation that is difficult or impossible to escape from.

a. *During the negotiations I was shocked when I realized I had painted myself into a corner.*
b. *The company painted itself into a corner by promising early delivery on the product.*
c. *Don't paint yourself into a corner!*

Paint the town red

The color red is associated with anger, blood, sex and violence. In this expression it refers to going out to bars, cabarets, clubs and the like to celebrate in a boisterous fashion.

a. *When my friend got promoted he wanted to go out and paint the town red.*

b. *After the game the fan club went out and painted the town red.*
c. *We ran into a group of college students who were out painting the town red.*

Palm off something

This phrase comes from the tricks performed by magicians, especially in sleight of hand tricks. It means pretending that something is more valuable than it really is and using some kind of trickery or false information to sell it for more than it is worth, or get someone to take an unwanted item off your hands.

a. *If you are trying to palm off that thing on me, forget it! I'm not falling for that trick!*
b. *I tried to palm off a cheap watch by claiming it was a Rolex.*
c. *Don't try to palm something off on him. He's too smart for that.*

Pass the buck

This expression is apparently based on the word "buck," which is a slang term for one dollar, with a kind of twist. Instead of meaning pass (give) a dollar to someone, it means to avoid blame or responsibility for something.

a. *The foreman in that group is always passing the buck when something goes wrong.*
b. *If you don't stop passing the buck no one will ever trust you.*
c. *I tried to pass the buck but my girlfriend caught on instantly.*

Pat on the back

A "pat on the back" is an act of praising someone, and may be verbal or physical or both.

a. *People love getting a pat on the back, whether they deserve it or not.*
b. *The teacher made sure that every student who handed his or her homework in on time got a pat on the back.*
c. *Since nobody else has done it, I will pat myself on the back!*

Pay an arm and a leg

Losing an arm or a leg is a serious thing. This fact gave birth to the expression "pay an arm and a leg," meaning to pay a very high price for something.

a. *I paid an arm and a leg for my car, but I am not very happy with it.*
b. *They want an arm and a leg for their products.*
c. *My wife admitted that she had paid an arm and a leg for the new furniture.*

Pay dirt

"Pay dirt" is an old miner's term referring to dirt in which there are flakes or tiny pieces of gold or silver. When digging, miners would watch out for "pay dirt." Nowadays, pay dirt is used in reference to discovering or finding something valuable.

a. *We hit pay dirt when we got the rights to distribute the new product.*
b. *If we don't hit pay dirt soon we're going to have to close down.*
c. *At the very last moment, the company hit pay dirt.*

Pay off

The original meaning of "pay off" is to pay what you owe, but in recent time it has taken on the additional meaning of paying off someone for some illegal or immoral action, as in "bribe."

a. *The mayor was forced to resign from his position because he took a pay off from some construction company.*
b. *He said it was a gift, not a pay off.*
c. *The salesman kept hinting that there would be some kind of pay off if I gave him an order.*

Pay through the nose

Inserting something into the nose or withdrawing a tube or something from the nose can be painful. This gave birth to the expression "pay through the nose," meaning to pay a very high price, pay too much, for something.

a. *I had to pay through the nose for the painting because the artist had suddenly become famous.*
b. *It really bugs me when I have to pay through the nose for something.*
c. *Don't pay through the nose for that! Shop around!*

Pecking order

In the chicken and fowl kingdom there is always a pecking order in any group, with those who peck and those who get pecked. "Pecking order" refers to a similar situation among people.

a. *I learned the pecking order in the company after having been there for less than a week.*
b. *The pecking order in the company was very precise and rigidly enforced.*
c. *It is uncomfortable to work in a company that has such a strong pecking order.*

Peter out

A slang term that came from the mining industry, peter out means to diminish gradually, to become exhausted. It is now commonly used in business and in private life to express these meanings.

a. *I'm petered out! I'm going home and going to bed!*
b. *Let's stop for a few minutes. I'm all petered out!*
c. *Our sales began to peter out right after Christmas.*

Pick the brains

Asking questions of others in order to learn from them is known as "picking their brains." This process is very common, but it sometimes has negative connotations when people depend on picking the brains of others rather than studying or doing their own research.

a. *Every time I get near that guy he tries to pick my brain.*
b. *Most people don't mind having their brains picked.*
c. *Many people try to save time, money and energy by picking the brains of others.*

Piece of cake

Something that is very easy to do; deriving from the fact that cake is "easy to eat" because of a natural fondness for sweet things.

a. *At first I was worried, but the new job turned out to be a piece of cake!*
b. *Getting my driver's license was a piece of cake.*
c. *She said finding her house would be a piece of cake.*

Piece of the action

Getting a "piece of the action" refers to getting some of the profits of some kind of activity. The activity may or may not be legitimate.

a. *He promised to give me a piece of the action in exchange for my advice.*
b. *I found out later that several outsiders were getting a piece of the action.*
c. *He threatened to expose the operation if he did not get a piece of the action.*

Pig in a poke

Poke is a slang term for a paper bag, and obviously once you put something in a paper bag you can no longer see it. This expression derived from the idea of buying a pig without first seeing it. It is now used in reference to a concept or thing that cannot be visually inspected.

a. *Don't expect me to agree to a pig in a poke! If you want me to buy your old computer let me see it first.*
b. *Going on a blind date is a pig in a poke experience!*
c. *Don't expect me to accept a pig in a poke!*

Pillar of society

Someone who makes extraordinary contributions to society is often referred to as "a pillar of society." In other words, he or she supports society the way pillars support buildings.

a. *Rich men and women often become pillars of society in their old age.*

b. *You can certainly say that Bill Gates is a pillar of society.*
c. *You don't have to be rich to become a pillar of society.*

Play ball

Of course, play ball actually means play ball. It also means to cooperate, to accept the position or proposals of others, to "get with" the group or the team.

a. *Look! If you don't play ball with us this deal is not going to go through!*
b. *You said he was ready to play ball!*
c. *When you're ready to play ball let me know.*

Play by ear

Some people learn how to play the piano or some other musical instrument by listening to and remembering the sounds, rather than by reading musical notes. This gave rise to the saying, "play by ear." Now, the expression is also used in reference to reacting to events or situations without any particular planning.

a. *I'm not sure if I will do anything this holiday. I'm just playing it by ear.*
b. *I have no plans for tomorrow. I'm just playing it by ear.*
c. *Forget making plans. Let's play it by ear. It's more interesting that way.*

Play cat-and-mouse with someone

When cats catch mice they will normally "play with them" or "tease them" for several minutes before killing and eating them. This characteristic gave rise to the expression "play cat and mouse" with someone, meaning teasing or fooling them in some way.

a. *It only took a few minutes for me to realize he was playing cat and mouse with me.*
b. *Every time I tried to pin her down she went into her cat and mouse routine.*
c. *This is not the time to be playing cat and mouse!*

Play hard to get

Resisting the advances or entreaties of someone, to tease them, or to get a better deal; especially used in reference to women, is referred to as playing hard to get.

a. *Playing hard to get comes natural to many women.*
b. *Don't give up. She's just playing hard to get.*
c. *If you play too hard to get you may lose out in the end.*

Play hardball

Playing ball very aggressively, far more aggressively than normal, is often described as playing hard ball. The expression is now used to describe other situations where the tactics of the individuals are especially strong.

a. *The lawyer they hired came out playing hardball.*
b. *As soon as the negotiations started I knew the other side was going to play hardball.*
c. *Look! If you want to win you'd better start playing hardball.*

Play into one's hands

This expression probably came from playing cards, when players would lay down cards that give their opponents and advantage. It is now used in many other situations.

a. *When the batter lost his temper he played into the hands of the pitcher.*
b. *The salesman played into my hands when he gave me the price in advance.*
c. *We must not do anything that would play into their hands.*

Play second fiddle

In an orchestra the man who plays second fiddle is normally junior in both skill and seniority to the lead fiddler. The prestige of the position is therefore lower and less desirable.

a. *That senior vice president says he will never play second fiddle to a new president.*
b. *Some people are just not cut out to play second fiddle.*
c. *I don't mind playing second fiddle to him. He is an outstanding manager.*

Play the innocent

Act like you are innocent; that you don't know anything about something, especially in reference to a legal matter, a game of chance or in male-female relations.

a. *Women who work in cabarets often play the innocent because they know it appeals to men.*
b. *He's a sucker for a girl who plays the innocent.*
c. *We might get by with it if we play the innocent.*

Play the martyr

Sacrifice one's self in order to get sympathy, or because of lack of self-confidence and a desire to be appreciated and liked.

a. *Women often end up playing the martyr, especially in catering to their children.*
b. *Don't play the martyr with me!*
c. *If you want to play martyr you will be the loser!*

Playing with house money

"House money" is money that doesn't belong to you; that belongs to the casino, for example, and is given to you to gamble with, so if you lose it's no big deal. It is also used in the sense that you may as well try something that is risky if you are not using your own money.

a. *Politicians love to finance big projects because they are playing with house money!*
b. *You're using house money so go ahead and take a chance.*
c. *You act like you're playing with house money.*

Polish the apple

Apples that are going to be given away are often polished to make them look more attractive. This custom led to the expression "polish the apple," meaning to flatter someone.

a. *Our manager was too tough. He didn't respond to attempts to polish the apple.*
b. *Some students attempt to get in good with their teachers by polishing the apple.*
c. *Taking apples to your teacher is a very direct way of polishing the apple.*

Pour cold water on it

Pouring cold water on something obviously takes some of the heat out of it; just as a cold shower reduces a sudden surge of sexual passion. Pouring cold water on an idea takes the form of criticizing it.

a. *Every time I come up with a new idea, you pour cold water on it!*
b. *Stop pouring cold water on everything I suggest!*
c. *He poured cold water on the best idea I've ever had!*

Pull a fast one

"Pulling a fast one" on someone means to cheat them, to "fake them out," to do something unexpected that gives you an advantage.

a. *Our chief competitor pulled a fast one by introducing a new product two months earlier than we expected.*
b. *As soon as I heard the news I knew he had pulled a fast one on me.*
c. *That company is notorious for pulling fast ones when it comes to new designs.*

Pull off

"Pull off" refers to succeeding in doing something that is difficult, that was believed impossible, or that is surprising for some reason.

a. *The conman pulled off a scam that you wouldn't believe.*

b. *If you can pull that off I will be surprised.*
c. *The computer company pulled off a coup with its new product.*

Pull out of a hat

Magicians are known for pulling rabbits out of hats. If you do something that is totally unexpected, that appears magical, it may be described as having been pulled out of a hat.

a. *When it looked like the talks were going to fail we managed to pull a solution out of the hat.*
b. *The basketball player pulled a move out of the hat that I had never seen before.*
c. *If you are depending on him to pull success out of a hat you may be disappointed.*

Pull the wool over the eyes

Pulling a woolen cap over one's eyes makes it impossible to see, and is used to mean misleading someone about something.

a. *He tried to pull the wool over her eyes, but she was on to him.*
b. *That rat really pulled the wool over my eyes!*
c. *He's an expert at pulling the wool over people's eyes.*

Pulling my leg

I don't know how this expression came about, but it is used to mean teasing, especially telling a fictional story as if it were true just to get someone to fall for it (accept it as true).

a. *There's no way that could be true! You're pulling my leg, aren't you?*
b. *He was just pulling her leg!*
c. *You shouldn't pull his leg like that! He takes it seriously!*

Push back the clock

As the saying goes, time waits for no one, but people are always trying to delay the passing of time, to "push back the clock," in order to accomplish something when there is little or no time left.

a. *If we're going to get this job done we're going to have to push back the clock!*
b. *This has been a great vacation. I wish we could push back the clock.*
c. *That guy is so lazy he's always trying to push back the clock.*

Put a lid on it

Putting a lid on a pot or barrel or some other type of container is usually the last step in some process. In colloquial use, putting a lid on something refers to ending or stopping something, from a speech to a rumor that is going around.

a. *I don't care how you do it but put a lid on that rumor!*
b. *That's not music; it's just noise, so put a lid on it.*
c. *Your yapping is driving me crazy! Put a lid on it!*

Put a sock in it

This phrase may have come from the use of "socked in" to mean that the view is obscured by bad weather. In colloquial use it means to stop talking; to figuratively put a sock in your mouth.

a. *Enough already! Put a sock in it!*
b. *When she started to sing someone yelled: "Put a sock in it!"*
c. *That guy is so boring! I wish he would put a sock in it!*

Put all of your eggs in one basket

If you put all of your eggs in one basket and then drop it they may all be broken, thus doing so is a risk or gamble.

a. *If you go on only one job interview you will be putting all of your eggs in one basket!*
b. *If you buy just one stock you may be putting all of your eggs in one basket.*
c. *With more than one product we won't have all of our eggs in one basket.*

Put in two cents worth

"Put in two cents worth" refers to expressing an opinion that may not be important, or that one wants to play down as unimportant.

a. *If I may be allowed to put in my two cents worth, I suggest that we junk this deal.*
b. *When he put his two cents worth in everybody laughed.*
c. *They told me my two cents wasn't worth one cent!*

Put on one's thinking cap

This expression comes from the wish that there was, in fact, some kind of "thinking cap" device we could put on our heads to make us smarter.

a. *Before starting the test I went through a mental exercise of putting on my thinking cap.*
b. *When I asked him I could almost see him putting on his thinking cap.*
c. *Put on your thinking cap and explain this to me.*

Put one's cards on the table

This expression is taken from the game of cards, and refers to letting someone know your attitude, your position, honestly and completely, not holding anything back.

a. *If you put your cards on the table too soon you are in trouble!*
b. *I never put my cards on the table when I am dealing with him.*
c. *Let's both put our cards on the table and get this over with!*

Put one's foot in one's mouth

This expression may come from the fact that trying to put your foot in your mouth would be an awkward, embarrassing and ultimately impossible thing to do. It refers to getting into a jam or some kind of trouble by saying something wrong, embarrassing or rude.

a. *Every time she opens her mouth she puts her foot in it.*
b. *As soon as I made the statement I knew I had put my foot in my mouth.*
c. *If you can't talk without putting your foot in your mouth it is better to say nothing.*

Put our heads together

This expression is based on the idea that "two heads are better than one"—meaning that two people conferring together are more likely to come up with a better or correct solution.

a. *If we put our heads together we can work this out.*
b. *They put their heads together and came up with a solution in just a few minutes.*
c. *The Japanese are known for putting their heads together to solve problems.*

Put out to pasture

When a horse, mule or other draft animal becomes too infirm or too old to work (or race) it may be "put out to pasture," meaning that it is allowed to live out its life grazing and taking it easy in a field. The phrase is also used in reference to older employees.

a. *As soon as employees in that company reach 60 they are put out to pasture.*
b. *My boss said I was being put out to pasture.*
c. *It's not fair to put employees out to pasture when they are still able to work.*

Put the brakes on

Of course, when you put the brakes on in a moving vehicle, it slows down or stops. This expression refers to a slow-down or stoppage of anything, from trying to "make out" with the opposite sex to a political campaign or the design of a new product.

a. *You're rushing that girl! You'd better put the brakes on!*
b. *We had to put the brakes on launching the marketing program.*
c. *The word came down for us to put the brakes on the new product design.*

Put the cart before the horse

Obviously if you put a cart in front of a horse the horse can't pull it. This expression thus refers to doing things in the wrong order.

a. *That's putting the cart before the horse! It will never work!*
b. *He has a bad habit of always putting the cart before the horse.*

c. *It was all I could do to prevent myself from putting the cart before the horse in my dealings with her.*

Put the welcome mat out

Some homes have a foot mat at the entrance that is inscribed with the word WELCOME. When you "put the welcome mat out," you make special arrangements to greet and cater to someone.

a. *The welcome mat is always out at his house.*
b. *The president put the welcome mat out for the visiting prime minister.*
c. *She became a famous hostess by putting a welcome mat out for everyone.*

Put two and two together

Putting "two and two together" refers to making a correct guess or making a correct analysis of a situation.

a. *The police very quickly put two and two together and identified the thief.*
b. *We were able to put two and two together and quickly discovered the problem.*
c. *All we have to do is put two and two together to find the answer.*

Put up a good fight

The original meaning of this expression is, of course, clear. It now also refers to putting up a good struggle or good show in any kind of game, contest, business competition, and so on.

a. *We put up a good fight before losing to a larger company.*
b. *She put up a good fight when I told her she couldn't go.*
c. *It won't do you any good to put up a good fight. You have already lost!*

Put up a good front

A "good front" is an appearance or behavior that is impressive, that makes a good impression.

a. *The job applicant put up a good front, but once hired he proved to be a very poor worker.*
b. *He bought a new suit in order to put up a good front at his interview.*
c. *It was obvious she was trying to put up a good front.*

Put up or shut up

People who talk a lot and make a lot of promises without ever delivering them may be told to put up or shut up.

a. *Just once I wish that guy would put up or shut up! All he does is talk!*
b. *Why don't you tell him to put up or shut up.*
c. *When I hedged about getting married she told me to put up or shut up.*

Put words into one's mouth

"Putting words into another person's mouth" refers to saying what you think another person would say or said about something. Doing this has negative implications because it is generally difficult or impossible to know exactly what the other person said or might say.

a. *Stop putting words in my mouth! I can speak for myself!*
b. *He has a very bad habit of putting words into other people's mouths.*
c. *I don't mean to put words in your mouth, but don't you agree with me!*

Put your best foot forward

This commonly used phrase means that in any endeavor you should always do the best that you can by emphasizing your most attractive and strongest attributes.

a. *If you are serious about getting that new job you had better put your best foot forward!*
b. *You say you put your best foot forward and still couldn't make time with that girl!*
c. *Well maybe your best foot forward isn't good enough for her!*

Put your foot down

When people decide to suddenly begin enforcing some custom that is being ignored or rule of law that is being broken, it may be described as "putting their foot down"—in other words, taking a firm stand.

a. *The government should put its foot down in the case of illegal immigrants.*
b. *If you keep that up I'm going to put my foot down!*
c. *When the police department put its foot down the mugging stopped.*

Put your heart into it!

Putting your heart into something means to try harder, to give it everything you have. In other words, to extend yourself as far as your heart will allow.

a. *We're not going to win this game if you don't put your heart into it!*
b. *When you make love to her/him you'd better put your heart into it!*
c. *She puts her heart into everything she does!*

Quit while you are ahead

In gambling and other endeavors, it often happens that one does quite well at the beginning, but the longer you play or persist the more likely you are to lose. So this admonition is to stop before you begin to lose.

a. *You've made your point. I suggest you quit while you are ahead.*
b. *He should have quit when he was ahead.*
c. *Some people just can't quit even when they are ahead.*

Rack one's brain

The word "rack" has several meaning and uses, including that of a torture device used to stretch a victim's body, causing extreme pain and serious injury to the body if done to an extreme. "Rack one's brain," an offshoot of this shocking custom, means to strain very hard to think of something, to remember something.

a. *I racked my brain for over an hour trying to figure out what to do about a computer problem.*
b. *Instead of racking your brain, look it up in a dictionary or ask someone!*
c. *Day after day the engineers racked their brains in an effort to improve the design.*

Rain check

This was originally a ticket stub for an outdoor sports event entitling the holder to admission at a future date if the event was cancelled because of rain. Now it refers to postponing acceptance of any offer.

a. *I'm tied up tomorrow. How about a rain check on your invitation to lunch?*
b. *If you don't mind I'll take a rain check on that.*
c. *She always takes a rain check when you invite her out!*

Ram down someone's throat

The image of ramming something down someone's throat is very unpleasant. The expression means to force someone to agree to something they don't agree with or approve of.

a. *When he tried to ram his theory down my throat I simply ignored him.*
b. *If you try to ram it down their throats they will become more uncooperative.*
c. *Don't try to ram it down their throats! Persuade them?*

Rat race

Rats are known to rush around endlessly, giving birth to the phrase "rat race" in reference to a lifestyle that is too fast, too all-consuming, and often seems to have no worthwhile purpose.

a. *He got so tired of his daily rat race that he retired at the age of 50 and moved into a cabin in the countryside.*

b. *I could tell that the rat race was driving her crazy. She was so uptight it was driving me crazy!*
c. *Many people are still caught in the rat race when they are in their seventies.*

Raw deal

"Raw" originally referred to uncooked meat. It then came to mean things that were unfinished, that were unpleasant, or cruel and painful. A "raw deal" is a deal that is unfair, unpleasant, painful, etc.

a. *I got a raw deal when I bought a used car.*
b. *If you think you got a raw deal you should hear what happened to me!*
c. *Breaking up with your girlfriend that way was a raw deal.*

Read between the lines

If you are able "to read between the lines" it means you understand more than what is written down or said.

a. *If you can't read between the lines that guy will take advantage of you.*
b. *She sounded sincere but reading between the lines told a different story.*
c. *Being able to read between the lines is something like mind-reading.*

Read the riot act

Reading the riot act has nothing to do with riots. It has to do with telling somebody off; with criticizing them; with telling them what they did wrong; a warning.

a. *The new police chief read the riot act to the rowdy students.*
b. *My mother was an expert at reading the riot act to me when I was young.*
c. *Somebody should read the riot act to those striking workers.*

Red cent

A red cent used to refer to a coin with the smallest value, and eventually came to mean a very small sum of money.

a. *I wouldn't give a red cent for that old car!*
b. *When it comes to work, he's not worth a red cent.*
c. *Sorry! I don't have a red cent on me.*

Red herring

In the old days, a dead red herring was used to distract hunting dogs away from some scent, giving rise to the expression "a red herring," meaning an unimportant matter that draws attention away from the main subject.

a. *Every time I brought up the subject of pay, the manager brought up a red herring.*
b. *It was obvious that the speech was nothing more than a red herring.*
c. *Both lawyers and politicians are experts at introducing red herrings into their presentations.*

Red-letter day

The color red is closely associated with things that are important and attractive, resulting in the expression "a red-letter day" referring to a day that is memorable because of some important event.

a. *It was a red-letter day when she finally received her graduation diploma.*
b. *The opening of the new plant was a red-letter day.*
c. *The arrival of the prime minister at the school was a red-letter day for the students.*

Ride herd on

"Ride herd on" is an expression that comes from the world of cattle and cowboys. Cowboys rode horses to keeps herds of cattle under control and move them around. It means to watch closely and control.

a. *He knew that if he didn't ride herd on his employees they would not get the job done in time.*
b. *We have to ride herd on this project to make sure it is done right.*
c. *I don't want to ride herd on you! I want you to be responsible for yourself.*

Ring down the curtain

This old theater expression refers to the end of an act when the curtain is lowered. Now it is used to indicate the ending of any action or event.

a. *The manager told us to ring down the curtain on the new marketing program.*
b. *The singer was so bad they rang the curtain down on her.*
c. *Let's not ring the curtain down before we have a chance to test the product.*

Roll out the red carpet

The color red has long been associated with high rank and royalty, giving birth to the expression "roll out the red carpet," meaning to spread a red carpet on the ground for some dignitary to walk on as a show of respect.

a. *The welcoming committee made arrangements for a red carpet to be rolled out to the president's plane.*
b. *I felt like a celebrity when they rolled out a red carpet to welcome me.*
c. *It was decided to give the new company president the red carpet treatment when he arrived.*

Roll up one's sleeves

"Rolling up one's sleeves" has long been common a custom among men engaged in heavy, hot work. When used as an expression its meaning changes to getting ready to engage in some hard, demanding work.

a. *Let's roll up our sleeves and get this work done before the end of the day.*
b. *The workmen were impressed when the foreman rolled up his sleeves and joined them.*
c. *Here comes the boss! Roll up your sleeves and act busy!*

Rubbing elbows with someone

This expression refers to being at a meeting, party or reception where there are a lot of people and you have an opportunity to meet and talk with them. Many such meetings are arranged specifically for that purpose, and in some cases are called "mixers," since you get to "mix" with others.

a. *I especially wanted to go to the annual party so I could rub elbows with the top managers of the company.*
b. *At the convention I was able to rub elbows with several famous inventors.*
c. *Let's go in and see how many good-looking women we can rub elbows with.*

Run around in circles

Obviously, if you run around in circles, you never get beyond the circle. So this expression refers to being very active, very busy, but not accomplishing anything—an apt description of some employees in companies.

a. *Let's change our strategy. All we've been doing is run around in circles!*
b. *He looks busy but he's just running around in circles.*
c. *Let's keep them running around in circles until we figure out how to deal with them!*

Run like a scared rabbit

Rabbits are timid creatures and run at the slightest hint of any danger. The saying is also applied to people.

a. *When the bully started across the street I ran like a scared rabbit.*
b. *Come on! Don't act like a scared rabbit! Those guys are really cute!*
c. *Acting like a scared rabbit won't get you anywhere!*

Run short

To "run short" means to not have enough of something; to not have enough of something to continue or to finish something.

a. *We ran short of gas when we were still miles from our destination.*
b. *The company ran short of funds.*
c. *If you don't control your spending you will run short of money.*

Sacred cow

A "sacred cow" is a person or thing that is not or cannot be criticized or changed because it is under some kind of special protection, is seen as absolutely indispensable.

a. *The subsidized school lunch program has become a sacred cow and nobody would dare try to change it.*
b. *In the world of politics there are many sacred cows.*
c. *The professor began to act like he was a sacred cow.*

Saddled with debt

The word "saddle" refers to the leather seat put on a horse to make it easier for the rider. It also refers to putting a burden on someone and to encumber them with some obligation.

a. *If you continue spending like that you are going to be saddled with debt.*
b. *The company became so saddled with debt the owners had to sell it.*
c. *Being saddled with debt is a terrible thing.*

Salt away

Salt is a well-know preservative, so it is not surprising that "salt away" refers to "preserving" (saving) money.

a. *My father's uncle salted away thousands of dollars before he died.*
b. *If you don't start salting some money away you're going to be in trouble.*
c. *He was notorious for salting away everything he got his hands on.*

Save for a rainy day

In this case, a rainy day refers to a time when you will need something, such as money to pay for an emergency or some other special need.

a. *Some people never think of saving for a rainy day.*
b. *You'd better start saving for a rainy day!*
c. *We were too poor to save for a rainy day.*

Save one's breath

If someone tells you to "save your breath" they are telling you to keep quiet; that whatever it is you might say won't do any good.

a. *You can save your breath and not bother talking to him. He never listens to anyone.*
b. *I was tempted to save my breath but I spoke up anyway.*
c. *I wanted to tell him to save his breath but I didn't have a chance. He spoke up too quickly.*

Save one's neck

This expression is derived from the practice of hanging people by the neck as a form of execution, so "saving your neck" or someone else's neck has come to mean saving someone from some kind of problem or danger, including making a fool of themselves.

a. *She saved my neck by telling me that the president was going to visit our department that morning.*
b. *He tried to save his neck by lying about his responsibility for the accident.*
c. *I've saved your neck for the last time! From now on you're on your own!*

Saved by the bell

One story of how this expression came to be is that our ancestors realized that they were burying people before they were actually dead, and came up with a solution. They tied a string to the "dead" person's hand, buried him then tied the other end of the string to a bell hung on a nearby tree branch. If the person revived enough to ring the bell, their survivors would rush out and dig them up—hence "saved by the bell." Of course, another story is that the saying came from boxing, where ringing a bell ended a round of fighting, and often saved boxers from being defeated in that particular round of fighting.

a. *The stocks would have gone down further but they were saved by the bell.*
b. *You can't always expect to be saved by the bell.*
c. *Students who haven't done their homework may hope to be saved by the bell.*

Say with a straight face

This saying refers to someone telling a lie or telling some kind of outlandish story without any expression on his or her face in order to make the story more believable.

a. *He told me the same goofy story with a straight face!*
b. *You told that crazy story with a straight face?*
c. *I knew I had to keep a straight face or she wouldn't believe me.*

Scratch one's back

Having your back scratched can feel awfully good, thus the various "scratch one's back" expressions. They mostly refer to doing something kind or helpful for someone in the hope that they will return the favor in the future.

a. *You scratch my back and I'll scratch yours!*
b. *If you want to get in good books with that company you have to do a lot of back-scratching.*
c. *We were both bent on scratching each other's back, so we got along great.*

See eye to eye

Seeing "eye to eye" has come to mean having the same opinion or opinions as someone else, or fully agreeing with someone on something.

a. *My wife and I never see eye to eye on which TV show to watch.*
b. *I was very pleased to learn that the new man and I saw eye to eye on most things.*
c. *If we can't see eye to eye on this let's forget it.*

See red

"See red" refers to becoming angry, and the expression either grew out of the association of the color red with blood and violence, or the fact that the faces of some people flush red when they become angry.

a. *When I heard what had happened I saw red, and had difficulty controlling myself.*

b. *If you say that, he is going to see red. He can't stand criticism.*
c. *The hecklers made the speaker see red when they continued to interpret him.*

Seeing the light

"Seeing the light" refers to reaching a point where you are quite sure you are going to succeed—where you can see the light of success—or, the point where you finally understand something, whether good or bad.

a. *Management assured us that we would be seeing the light within six months.*
b. *I finally saw the light and confessed that it was my fault.*
c. *If we don't see the light soon this project is going to be history.*

Seize the moment

This very common saying refers to taking advantage of an opportunity the moment it appears. It implies that the opportunity may not last long so it is wise to seize in quickly.

a. *My boss paid me a compliment so I seized the moment and asked for a raise!*
b. *Success in business often means knowing when to seize the moment.*
c. *She seized the moment to criticize his drinking.*

Sell like hotcakes

The popularity of hotcakes results in them selling exceptionally well, giving rise to "selling like hotcakes" being used in reference to any item that sells especially well.

a. *Just before Christmas toys for children sell like hotcakes.*
b. *The new electronic device began selling like hotcakes the day it appeared on the market.*
c. *The new item sold like hotcakes for a few days, and then died.*

Set back

To set something back is to impede the progress or advance of something, causing a delay or forcing something to stop altogether.

a. *The change in the currency rate was a serious set back for the company.*
b. *In this business you have to be ready at all times for a set back.*
c. *The project was set back by bad weather.*

Seven-year itch

In American folk lore, husbands and wives tend to become tired of each other in their seventh year of marriage, and that is when one or the other may begin "itching" to have an affair with someone else.

a. *In some marriages the seven-year itch begins after just two or three years.*
b. *You act like you are suffering from the seven-year itch!*
c. *Some people come down with the seven-year itch just after their honeymoon!*

Shake a leg!

This rather odd but common expression is a request or order to speed things up, to walk faster, work faster or whatever.

a. *You're getting behind! Shake a leg!*
b. *Tell her to shake a leg!*
c. *If you don't shake a leg we'll never get there!*

Shape up or ship out

Ship out is, of course, an old nautical term referring to leaving on a ship, and shape up means to put things, or yourself, in order. In common use today the phrase means start doing things right, or get out; leave.

a. *You may be the boss' son, but you'd better shape up or ship out!*
b. *I was shocked when she told me to shape up or ship out.*
c. *His boss gave him no choice. He had to shape up or ship out.*

Sharp as a tack

Someone who is especially smart, clever, quick to understand may be referred to as "sharp as a tack."

a. *That new secretary is as sharp as a tack.*
b. *You have to be as sharp as a tack to work for that company.*
c. *You could tell he was as sharp as a tack the moment he opened his mouth.*

Sharp cookie

Someone who is very intelligent and very quick mentally is often referred to as being "a sharp cookie," probably because cookies are especially tasty and "hit the spot."

a. *Everyone in that software company is a sharp cookie.*
b. *That girl is determined to marry a sharp cookie.*
c. *To get into that company you have to be a sharp cookie and aggressive!*

She has him twisted around her little finger

Said of a woman who controls the behavior of a man, more or less like a string around her finger.

a. *She has her husband twisted around her little finger.*
b. *She is a master at twisting men around her little finger.*
c. *I'm not going to let you twist me around your little finger.*

Shoe is on the other foot

"Shoe on the other foot" refers to a situation which turns out to be the opposite of what it originally was, or was said to be by someone.

a. *My friend laughed when I told him I was in the dog house with my wife. Now the shoe is on the other foot. His wife won't let him in the house!*
b. *He accused me of spreading rumors. Now I know the shoe is on the other foot.*
c. *The clerk accused the customer of stealing. It turned out that the shoe is on the other foot.*

Shot in the arm

This expression apparently comes from the fact that some substances injected into the bloodstream of a person gives them a energy boost or makes them feel better in some way. It refers to something that is energizing, encouraging, inspiring.

a. *The opinion polls were a shot in the arm for the mayor's campaign.*
b. *The hot tea acted like a shot in the arm.*
c. *This product needs a shot in the arm.*

Shove it up your ass!

A vulgar expression used when someone gets so fed up and frustrated that they use it to mean forget it; I'm not buying; I quit; to hell with you, and so on.

a. *I can't take this job any more, so you can shove it up your ass!*
b. *He can shove it up his ass as far as I'm concerned!*
c. *Imagine my surprise when she told me to shove it up my ass!*

Show one's true colors

"One's true colors" refers to his or her real character, to what one really feels and believes in, as opposed to their "public face."

a. *At the first setback in the negotiations, the leader showed his true colors by becoming angry and shouting.*
b. *I deliberately provoked him to see if he would show his true colors.*
c. *It didn't take long for her true colors to come out.*

Silver platter

In earlier times some very wealthy families were served their meals on silver platters. This custom resulted in receiving something that wasn't truly earned being described as "getting it on a silver platter."

a. *His job was handed to him on a silver platter by his uncle.*
b. *The new contract was handed to us on a silver platter.*
c. *You have to remember you can't get everything handed to you on a silver platter.*

Sitting duck

A sitting duck can be shot easily, giving rise to the expression "sitting duck" in reference to people and things who are vulnerable to being mistreated, attacked, exposed or otherwise the victim of something unpleasant or seriously damaging.

a. *When he went public with his views he became a sitting duck for everyone who disagreed with him.*
b. *I don't want to put myself in a position of being a sitting duck.*
c. *If you don't want to be a sitting duck, keep your head down and your mouth shut.*

Six of one and half a dozen of another

This saying is often used when there are two propositions or two positions that are so close to being identical that you can't tell them apart.

a. *What you just said is six of one and half a dozen of another! That's not a choice!*
b. *It doesn't make any difference. They're all six of one and half a dozen of another.*
c. *Come on! No more of this six of one and half a dozen of the other bullshit!*

Slings and arrows

The original reference of slings and arrows was to weapons used in fighting. Now it is used in reference to criticism of something or somebody.

a. *Politicians and executives often have to endure the slings and arrows of their critics.*
b. *I wouldn't mind the slings and arrows if they were honest, but they're not.*
c. *As soon as the new president was sworn in his enemies began bringing out their slings and arrows.*

Slip of the tongue

A "slip of the tongue" is saying something that you hadn't planned on saying, should not have said, or often would like to "take back."

a. *Telling him about the surprise party was a slip of the tongue.*
b. *Politicians often disavow what they say by claiming it was a slip of the tongue*
c. *He sometimes reveals confidential information on purpose by acting like it is a slip of the tongue.*

Smell blood

Sharks and land predators can smell blood from long distances, and immediately head in that direction looking for prey. In the colloquial sense, "smelling blood" means sensing an opportunity to achieve some goal; to win.

a. *You could tell after the first round that the boxer smelled blood!*

b. *He acts like a shark that has smelled blood.*
c. *I think the smell of blood turns you on!*

Smile when you say that

In old Western movies, heroes were often depicted as reacting to criticism or other harsh remarks by warning the villain that he had better smile to demonstrate that he was just joking...to avoid being shot.

a. *Alright! I'm overweight, but you'd better smile when you say that!*
b. *If you want to keep your job you'd better smile when you tell him.*
c. *He smiled when he said it so I knew it was a friendly remark.*

Smooth over

To "smooth over" something means to make it smooth, and may refer to a path, a road, or a dispute between people or companies.

a. *If we don't smooth over our relations with our supplier we may be out of business.*
b. *That couple is always in the process of smoothing over their relationship.*
c. *There is an old saying that couple should smooth over their problems before going to bed.*

Snake in the grass

Snakes are known for hiding in the grass, which allows them to sneak up on prey without being seen. A person who masks his or her real character and aims is often compared to a snake just waiting to strike an unsuspecting victim.

a. *Marie's new boyfriend turned out to be a snake in the grass!*
b. *I head that the new department head is a snake in the grass.*
c. *He was exposed as a snake in the grass.*

Souped up

This odd but common expression may have come from the efforts of cooks to make their soup taste better by adding special ingredients. It means to add horsepower or greater speed to an automobile engine.

a. *He souped his old car up to the point that he began to win races.*
b. *Manufacturers never get tired of souping up their cars.*
c. *Boy! You're really souped up today, aren't you!*

Spare me the details

This is an expression used to stop someone from going into excessive detail, or dull or disturbing details, in some kind of explanation or presentation.

a. *Please spare me the details and let's get on with it!*
b. *Spare me the details! I don't want to know why!*
c. *Even though he told me to spare him the details he wanted to know all about it.*

Speak with a forked tongue

In the early history of America, native Indians frequently accused government and military leaders of speaking to them with a forked tongue. The expression speaking with a forked tongue became synonymous with telling lies.

a. *Politicians often speak with a forked tongue.*
b. *Don't you think I know when you are speaking with a forked tongue?*
c. *You can't believe what he says. He speaks with a forked tongue.*

Spill the beans

This colloquial expression refers to telling confidential matters or secrets to someone.

a. *Somebody spilled the beans and within hours it was all over the school.*
b. *If you tell her she will spill the beans for sure!*
c. *I really had to try hard to avoid spilling the beans.*

Split hairs

"Splitting a hair" is, or would be, a very difficult task because hairs are so small. When someone continues to emphasize and argue about very small unimportant points or differences of opinion it is known as "splitting hairs."

a. *My boss always starts splitting hairs when I try to talk to him about something important.*
b. *People who habitually split hairs are really frustrating to talk to.*
c. *Let's not try splitting hairs about this. It's a waste of time.*

Spread your wings

It is a big day when baby birds spread their wings and fly for the first time. Now the expression may be used to refer to new school graduates, on the verge of going out into the world on their own for the first time; or to anyone starting a new venture.

a. *To succeed in that company you have to really spread your wings.*
b. *Management wouldn't let the employees spread their wings, so it failed.*
c. *I wanted to get out of school as quickly as possible and spread my wings!*

Square one

The number one squared is still one, resulting in the use of the phase "square one" to mean the beginning or from the beginning. It is frequently used in reference to efforts or projects that have to be started over because of some failure.

a. *When the bottom dropped out of the stock market we were back to square one.*
b. *The meeting was going nowhere so we decided to go back to square one.*
c. *I knew that if we had to go back to square one it would be very costly.*

Squeaky wheel gets the grease

This expression derives from the time when wagons were common and the wheels had to be greased regularly to keep them from squeaking. Now it refers to people who complain the loudest usually being helped first just to shut them up.

a. *If you want to get some action, remember it's the squeaky wheel that gets the grease!*
b. *That loud-mouthed politician knows it's the squeaky wheel that gets the grease.*
c. *Some times you have to act like a squeaky wheel to get any attention.*

Stab in the back

The expression "stab in the back" refers to saying or doing something that causes some kind of serious harm to someone's reputation, position or ability to function normally.

a. *I was shocked when my so-called friend stabbed me in the back with some dirty rumors.*
b. *A lot of back-stabbing goes on in that office.*
c. *If you turn your back on him, he's likely to stab you in the back.*

Stand on one's own feet

"Stand on one's own feet" means to be independent, usually financially and in other matters as well.

a. *I have been standing on my own feet since I was 14 years old.*
b. *If you can't stand on your own feet how do you expect to survive?*
c. *Young people need to be taught to stand on their own feet.*

Stand one's ground

This is another military term, and refers, of course, to not giving up ground to one's enemy. In this usage it means to maintain and defend one's position.

a. *We have to stand our ground if we are going to win this lawsuit.*
b. *Be sure to tell our negotiators to stand their ground.*
c. *You can't win if you don't stand your ground.*

Stand up to him/her

It has long been one of the fundamental traits of Americans that they "stand up" for their rights, refusing to be intimated or mistreated by anybody.

a. *If you don't stand up to him he is going to continue mistreating you!*
b. *The next time he starts harassing you stand up to him.*
c. *He is absolutely ruthless so the people are afraid to stand up to him.*

Start/get the ball rolling

This saying no doubt comes from a game that involves rolling a ball. It is used in reference to starting some action or activity.

a. *Well, it's time to go to work. Let's get the ball rolling.*
b. *If we don't get the ball rolling soon we won't finish today.*
c. *If everybody is here let's get the ball rolling.*

Stay on your toes

This is a figure of speech that derives from being prepared to jump aside or run, usually to escape some kind of danger; also to be ready to take advantage of an opportunity the moment it appears.

a. *You will really have to stay on your toes to keep up with that hotshot!*
b. *Well, don't give up! Stay on your toes!*
c. *Try staying on your toes for a change!*

Step on someone's toes

This old and still popular expression means to do something that embarrasses, displeases or offends someone.

a. *I did my best not to step on anyone's toes, but my best wasn't good*

enough.
b. *He goes around deliberately stepping on people's toes.*
c. *Don't step on that guy's toes! He'll come back at you!*

Stew in one's own juice

"Stew" and "juice" suggest something hot that is cooked on a stove. The idea of stewing in one's own juice is therefore an unpleasant situation that you brought on yourself.

a. *You caused the problem, not me, so stew in your own juice!*
b. *He was caught in a lie and left to stew in his own juice.*
c. *If you don't want to stew in your own juice stay out of trouble.*

Stick in the mud

Both literally and figuratively, a stick stuck in the mud is something that is devoid of character and personality and is totally uninteresting. The saying is commonly applied to men or women who are dull and never do or say anything exciting.

a. *She said her Saturday night date was a stick in the mud!*
b. *Lighten up! Being a stick in the mud is not going to get you anywhere!*
c. *I think girls have special radar that tells them when a guy is a stick in the mud.*

Stick one's neck out

In the old days "sticking one's neck out" could mean your head might be chopped off. It still refers to doing something that is risky or dangerous.

a. *I will stick my neck out for you, but this is the last time!*
b. *Thank you for sticking your neck out for me by defending my position.*
c. *He stuck his neck out for me by recommending me for the job.*

Stick to your guns

Be willing to defend your rights or your position no matter what, especially in an argument or negotiating procedure.

a. *If you don't stick to your guns you are going to come off as a weakling!*
b. *To argue with him you have to learn how to stick to your guns.*
c. *He lost the debate when he began to waffle instead of sticking to his guns.*

Stick your nose in

Attempting to, or succeeding in, becoming involved in someone else's affairs or activities without being invited—and when you generally are not welcome—is "sticking your nose" into someone else's business.

a. *If you stick your nose into his business you may get it smashed!*
b. *She's always sticking her nose into my business!*
c. *Don't stick your nose into other people's problems.*

Stickler for facts

Someone who is very fact-oriented, and insists upon having "the facts" of a situation, of whatever kind, before taking any action.

a. *He is notorious for being a stickler for facts!*
b. *Some people are sticklers for facts; others aren't.*
c. *The boss is a stickler for facts, so be prepared.*

Straight from the horse's mouth

Something that is heard directly from the person who is responsible is said to come "straight from the horse's mouth."

a. *The story of the plant closing came straight from the horse's mouth.*
b. *I won't believe it until I hear it straight from the horse's mouth.*
c. *The word finally came down straight from the horse's mouth that we were all going to be laid off.*

Straight from the shoulder

This expression has come to mean acting and speaking in an open, honest way, especially about sensitive and serious matters.

a. *You can depend on him to speak straight from the shoulder.*
b. *He is so dishonest he doesn't know what "straight from the shoulder" means!*
c. *I really want to know the truth. Give it to me straight from the shoulder.*

Strapped for cash

This expression evolved from the old word "strapped" which means penniless—having no money at all. "Strapped for cash" means being out of money temporarily.

a. *Many people are strapped for cash well before payday.*
b. *I'm strapped for cash so I'm not going out tonight.*
c. *The company became so strapped for cash it had to close down.*

Strike it rich

This is another miner's team meaning to find gold, silver or some other valuable mineral—often suddenly and unexpectedly. The expression is now used in a general sense relating to sudden success with something that brings in a lot of money.

a. *My neighbor struck it rich with a new video game.*
b. *If you get that process patented you may strike it rich.*
c. *I struck it rich when I met you!*

Strike while the iron is hot

This expression is an extension of the fact that irons used to press clothing must be hot to be effective. In this case, you have a much better chance of success if you "strike while the iron is hot"—in other words, make your move at the most opportune time.

a. *Unexpected publicity about the product made it possible for the company to strike while the iron was hot.*
b. *If we don't do it soon and strike while the iron is hot we will fail.*
c. *One of the secrets of success is striking while the iron is hot.*

Stuffed shirt

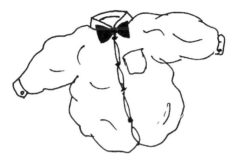

Shirts that are filled or stuffed with something appear stiff and rigid. This has developed into "stuffed shirt" meaning a person (usually a man) who is too formal, too rigid in his manner and attitudes.

a. *He is a classic stuffed shirt. You might as well get used to it.*
b. *Spending time with a stuffed shirt is boring; working with one is even worse.*
c. *Come on! Loosen up! Don't be a stuffed shirt!*

Sweep it under the rug

Sloppy housekeepers have been known to sweep dirt and other debris under a rug rather than pick it up and dispose of it outside. Politicians and others often sweep things under a rug (hide them) rather than deal with them forthrightly.

a. *He made every effort to sweep the growing scandal under the rug.*
b. *His first reaction was to sweep the problem under the rug.*
c. *Sweeping a problem under the rug is not a solution.*

Sweet on her/him

Using the word "sweet" in connection with male-female relations apparently comes from the fact that almost everybody likes sweets... so a sweetheart is someone you love. Being sweet on someone means to like or love them in a romantic sense.

a. *She is so sweet on him she can't even see anybody else.*
b. *I'm not sweet on her! She's just a friend!*
c. *From the way you act you are really sweet on her.*

Sweet times

"Sweet times" is similar to "good times" but has stronger implications; you might define it as meaning really good times or exceptionally good times.

a. *With the new contracts the company was soon enjoying some sweet times.*
b. *We can't always enjoy sweet times, so we have to try harder.*
c. *Looking back on the past year it was a period of sweet times.*

Sweetheart deal

A sweetheart is something that is very pleasing, very desirable, so "a sweetheart deal" is a business deal that is especially good.

a. *The company was saved from bankruptcy by a sweetheart deal with a foreign investor.*
b. *I hear you got a sweetheart deal with that company.*
c. *You're lucky to get a sweetheart deal like that.*

Swept off one's feet

This expression usually refers to feelings of happiness or love that are so strong you can't resist them and figuratively speaking "lose your balance."

a. *When I first saw her I was swept off my feet by her beauty.*
b. *When he was selected to be a pilot in the space program he was swept off his feet with pure joy.*
c. *The sight of the palace swept me off my feet.*

Take a back seat

The back seat of a vehicle, especially a bus or airplane, has long been regarded as the least desirable; as low class. Now the phrase is used to indicate virtually any position or thing that is less than the best.

a. *When it comes to computer skills he doesn't take a back seat to anyone!*
b. *I refuse to take a back seat to that goof-off.*
c. *That chef doesn't have to take a back seat to anyone.*

Take a beating

This is an obvious reference to being whipped or beaten, but in contemporary usage it refers to a loss of value or money.

a. *My friend took a beating on the stock market.*
b. *You may take a beating if you invest in real estate in that area.*
c. *The company took a beating when the new product failed to catch on.*

Take a breather

This is similar to "take a break," but more specifically it refers to stopping some action that is especially demanding so you can "catch your breath" by breathing deeply for a few minutes.

a. *This test is killing me. I need to take a breather!*
b. *As soon as you finish that you can take a breather.*
c. *When nearing the top of Mt. Fuji I had to take a breather every few steps.*

Take a nosedive

A "nosedive" refers to diving into the water—or the ground!—head or nose first, inferring that you go down very fast. The term is now used in reference to stock prices, the value of anything, one's reputation, etc., falling fast.

a. *When the news broke, the stock took a nosedive.*
b. *When the scandal broke, the CEO's reputation took a nosedive.*
c. *The market nosedived overnight.*

Take a number

In post offices and other places of business customers take a numbered slip from a dispensing machine so they will be served in the order of their arrival. This custom resulted in "take a number" being used as an expression in other situations as well.

a. *You get so many calls from boys! Why don't you have them take a number?*
b. *You want to kick my butt? Well take a number! There are several people ahead of you!*
c. *When I got to the post office I had to take a number.*

Take a page out of history

This expression refers to learning from history; learning from someone else's experience.

a. *The solution doesn't require rocket science. All we have to do is take a page out of history.*
b. *The fleet admiral won the battle by taking a page out of history.*
c. *If you want to succeed in politics you'd better take a page out of history.*

Take a run at it

Attempting to do something; especially something you have never done before.

a. *Well, I've never done that kind of work, but I'll take a run at it.*
b. *Okay. I'm willing to take a run at it if you are!*
c. *He said he would take a run at it.*

Take a spin/go for a drive

Go driving, usually on a short trip, for recreation or to check out a car that you might buy.

a. *When she offered to take me for a spin I jumped at the chance.*
b. *Before buying a car you should take it for a spin.*
c. *Many people like to go for a drive on weekends.*

Take a stand

To assume a position, either physically or intellectually, in some situation, in a fight, on questions of morality, politics, etc.

a. *You have to take a stand on this matter! You can't stay on the sidelines forever!*
b. *We are being sued so we have to take a stand.*
c. *Once my girlfriend takes a stand nothing will move her.*

Take care of number one

This expression came about from the custom of top corporate executives to give themselves large salaries, bonuses and other perks—in other words "taking care" of themselves first before considering their employees. The saying is now applied to anyone who selfishly puts himself or herself first.

a. *He is notorious for taking care of number one.*
b. *Executives who take care of number one first should not expect their employees to be loyal.*
c. *In that company you have to take care of number one because no one else will!*

Take it down a notch

A "notch" is the equivalent of a step or a narrow space. In this case, the expression is usually associated with measuring something, such as speed and sound.

a. *The music was so loud I asked them to take it down a notch.*
b. *Our advertising campaign is too hot. Let's take it down a notch.*
c. *She saw through my excuses, and proceeded to take me down a notch.*

Take it like a man

Accept the pain or a situation without complaining; said because Western males in particularly have traditionally been conditioned to believe that "real men" don't cry or become emotional.

a. *Many women can take it like a man—and more and more men are reacting like women!*
b. *When she was fired she took it like a man.*
c. *He told the little boy to take it like a man, but he cried anyway.*

Take it on the chin

This expression is from the world of boxing or fist-fighting, during which the participants often get hit on the chin. "Take it on the chin" means to get "hit" by some kind of trouble, to be willing to face something or somebody that has the potential for some kind of injury or unpleasant consequences.

a. *I knew I would have to take it on the chin in any encounter with him.*
b. *If you can't take it on the chin you won't make a good debater or a good lawyer.*
c. *The market has crashed so all we can do is take it on the chin and try to survive.*

Take it or leave it

An expression that means that's all there is; I'm not going to offer or give any more. If you don't accept, the deal, or whatever, is off.

a. *When he told me I had to take it or leave it, I left it!*
b. *That's my last offer. Take it or leave it!*
c. *It was one of those take it or leave it situations.*

Take off like a shot

Leave suddenly, quickly, in reference to the way a bullet leaves a gun barrel.

a. *When the man heard the police sirens he took off like a shot.*
b. *The instant the bell rang the students took off like a shot.*
c. *I was poised to take off like a shot at the first sign of danger.*

Take stock

Counting the items of merchandise or supplies that are in stock (on hand) is referred to as "taking stock." The term is also used in the sense of making a judgment or determination about matters or things in general.

a. *Before we do anything we had better take stock of our situation.*
b. *After taking stock of the company's situation we decided to cancel the merger.*
c. *Let's take stock of what we need before we going shopping.*

Take the bull by the horns

Cowboys who perform in rodeos grab the horns of cattle to wrestle them to the ground, and that may be the origin of the expression "take the bull by the horns." (It sounds possible!). It means to take some kind of decisive action, despite danger or opposition, in order to get something done.

a. *The manager decided to take the bull by the horns and get the project approved by the directors.*
b. *The new manager had a "take the bull by the horns" mentality, and it worked.*
c. *If we don't take the bull by the horns this project will never get off the ground floor.*

Take the high road

In this case, taking the high road means to choose the path or means that is morally superior.

a. *We should take the high road in all of our advertising.*
b. *We want to do business with a company that always takes the high road.*
c. *Many governments do not take the high road in their dealings with others.*

Take the sting out

Anyone stung by a bee knows that it feels better after the sting is pulled out. Taking the sting out of something refers to reducing the intensity, level or disturbing elements of one's comments or some action.

a. *The manager took the sting out of his comments by admitting that he had made similar mistakes.*
b. *She took some of the sting out of her criticism by smiling.*
c. *The termination bonus he received took some of the sting out.*

Take the wind out of one's sails

Stop someone from doing something; slow them down; shut them up.

a. *When the stock market crashed, it took the wind out of my sails!*
b. *When the teacher criticized her essay it took the wind out of her sails.*
c. *The wind went out of his sails when he heard her comment.*

Take time to smell the roses

Smelling a rose almost immediately improves one's mood and view of things in general. Many people now fail to take time out from work to smell the roses, that is, enjoy the many pleasures of life.

a. *I promised myself that I was going to take time to smell the roses, but I didn't.*
b. *The first thing I'm going to do is take time to smell the roses!*
c. *He has a "Take Time to Smell the Roses!" sign in his office.*

Take with a pinch of salt

Adding a bit of salt to food changes the taste, resulting in some things going down easier when you eat them. When you take something that somebody says "with a pinch of salt" it means you are not fully accepting what they say, because you cannot "swallow it."

a. *You must take everything he says with a pinch of salt.*
b. *If you take what he says with a pinch of salt it is not altogether so bad.*
c. *I will take that with a pinch of salt.*

Take your medicine

This expression has been extended to mean that someone who is guilty of something and deserves punishment should be willing to "take their medicine"—accept the punishment because in the end it will make them feel better.

a. *The smart choice is to take your medicine and get on with your life.*
b. *If he deserves to be punished he should take his medicine.*
c. *My dad told me to stand up and take my medicine.*

Taken for a ride

This is gangster talk for putting someone in a car, taking them somewhere and killing them. It is also used to mean being cheated out of something in a big way, especially by con artists.

a. *Many investors have been taken for a ride by companies that overstated their earnings.*
b. *Conmen are always looking for "marks" to take for a ride.*
c. *I fell for the scheme and was taken for a ride.*

Talk a good game

This remark is used in reference to someone who talks very knowledgeably about something, but actually is not that good at it. In other words, a person may talk a good baseball game but play the game poorly.

a. *He talks a good game but can he play?*
b. *Talking a good game is not the same as playing it!*
c. *You talk a good game but do you know how to play?*

Taste of one's own medicine

If you mistreat someone and they turn around and mistreat you it is often described as "getting a taste of your own medicine." The saying is virtually always used in a negative sense.

a. *She got a taste of her own medicine when other students started spreading rumors about her.*
b. *You'd better stop acting like that if you don't want to get a taste of your own medicine.*
c. *Some people never learn until they get a taste of their own medicine.*

Tell it like it is

Really tell the truth, regardless of the circumstances; especially in situations where the more common practice is to gloss over negative or unpleasant details.

a. *Travel authors and writers seldom really tell it like it is since they are selling tourism.*

b. *Don't give me that crap! Just tell it like it is!*
c. *I want the real truth! I want you to tell it like it is!*

Thankless job

A job that gives no satisfaction or is unpleasant for whatever reason is often described as "thankless."

a. *Working in a slaughterhouse has to be a thankless job.*
b. *A thankless job is better than none.*
c. *If you don't get an education you might end up with a thankless job.*

That doesn't ring a bell

This is a figurative way of saying that you have no memory of something; that you have no knowledge of it. In other words, a bell doesn't ring in your brain.

a. *I'm sorry. That name doesn't ring a bell.*
b. *Let me know if any of this rings a bell.*
c. *The sight of her rang a bell in my mind.*

That's a lot of crap!

"Crap" began as a losing hand in a dice game, and then took on the vulgar meaning of excrement (shit!) and the slang meaning of nonsense. In this expression, the meaning can be either excrement or nonsense.

a. *His whole speech was a lot of crap.*
b. *All I ever hear from you is a lot of crap!*
c. *Come on! Cut the crap and tell me the real story!*

That's a lot of crock

A crock is a large pot used to store things. In olden times, very large crocks were also used for holding and transporting liquids. In this saying, it refers to something that is not true (too big, too exaggerated, to be true).

a. *You know that's a lot of crock!*
b. *Over half of what he says is a lot of crock.*
c. *Do you expect me to believe that lot of crock?*

That's chicken feed

Chicken feed is small and not very impressive. A payment, salary or some kind of exchange that is exceptionally small is frequently referred to as chicken feed.

a. *You expect me to accept that salary! That's chicken feed!*
b. *A one dollar tip! That's not even chicken feed!*
c. *He said he was working for chicken feed.*

That's water under the bridge

After water has passed under a bridge, it is, of course, gone from that location forever. This saying infers that something is in the past and may as well be forgotten.

a. *Just as I predicted, their marriage is now water under the bridge.*
b. *Forget it! It's just water under the bridge!*
c. *She dismissed the whole thing by saying it was water under the bridge.*

The big picture

"The big picture" refers to a holistic or comprehensive view of something—how it works, what its overall impact is; what its results are likely to be.

a. *The company president was constantly accused of not seeing the big picture.*
b. *If we want to succeed in today's marketplace we have to see the big picture.*
c. *His obsession with seeing the big picture caused serious delays in launching the program.*

The bigger they are the harder they fall!

This is an old boxing expression, probably first said by a boxer facing a bigger opponent! It is now used in reference to the failure of companies, the downfall of high-ranked executives and politicians, etc.

a. *That boxer lives by the motto the bigger they are the harder they fall.*
b. *Company executives should keep in mind that the bigger they are the harder they fall.*
c. *He must have forgotten that the bigger you are the harder the fall.*

The blind leading the blind

When someone whose knowledge and experience is not adequate is leading, managing or teaching others who are in a similar situation, it is often referred to as the blind leading the blind.

a. *The new manager was so inexperienced it was a perfect example of the blind leading the blind.*
b. *I'm not qualified for that job. It would be the blind leading the blind.*
c. *As long as the blind are leading the blind the project will fail.*

The bottom fell out

When the bottom falls out of a bucket or some other container, whatever is in it goes down with the bottom. This phrase is now used in relation to markets, prices and stocks abruptly going down.

a. *The rumor caused the bottom to fall out of the stock market.*
b. *Just when the new product was introduced the bottom fell out of the market.*
c. *In just a matter of minutes the bottom fell out of the beef market.*

The bottom line

This phrase refers to the final outcome, profits, the end results, as well as the minimum that is acceptable.

a. *To save time, just give me your bottom line!*
b. *That company is more interested in the bottom line than in its customers.*
c. *The negotiators laid out their bottom line in bold terms.*

The die is cast

This saying evolved from the fact that after you pour hot metal into a cast, it cools, becomes hard, and generally cannot be changed. It is now commonly applied to decision-making.

a. *The president made the decision, so the die is cast.*
b. *The die is cast. There is nothing we can do about it.*
c. *Let's think about it some more before we cast the die.*

The early bird catches the worm

This commonsense saying can certainly be applied to human affairs as well as to birds.

a. *I followed the old adage that the early bird catches the worm, and was first in line for the new job.*
b. *My boss always comes to work early because he believes that the early bird catches the worm.*
c. *If you want to succeed in life, remember that it is the early bird that catches the worm.*

The fat is in the fire

When fat is tossed into a fire it burns quickly, causing flames to shoot up. This expression thus refers to something having been said or something having been done that may have an immediate and possibly dangerous effect.

a. *When the president said he was going to veto the bill, it was like throwing fat in the fire.*
b. *When I didn't answer her immediately it was like throwing fat in the fire.*
c. *As soon as I saw her face I knew the fat was in the fire.*

The one that got away

Originally this was a saying that fishermen used in claiming that they caught a really big fish but it got away. Now it is used in reference to opportunities lost or missed.

a. *When my friend was telling me about a girl he met he said she was the one that got away.*
b. *If you keep dwelling on the ones that got away you may never succeed.*
c. *We have to forget the ones that got away and look for new opportunities.*

The picture is/was bleak

This phrase refers to a situation that appears weak and gloomy, and not likely to turn out well. It is especially common in business, economic and political forecasts.

a. *When the economist was asked about the state of the nation his answer was blunt: "The picture is bleak!"*
b. *Well, even if the situation is bleak, let's do our best!*
c. *No matter which way you look at, the picture is bleak.*

The short end of the stick

This saying derives from the old custom of selecting partially concealed sticks of different lengths as a means of deciding winners and losers. The short stick designates the loser.

a. *Just my luck! I always get the short end of the stick!*
b. *When it comes to brains, he sure got the short end of the stick, didn't he?*
c. *Just make sure I don't get the short end of the stick!*

There is no accounting for taste

People differ in many ways, especially in their preference for food, giving rise to this common idiom, now applied to almost anything or any situation.

a. *When it comes to clothing styles there certainly is no accounting for taste.*
b. *You have no accounting for taste in clothing!*
c. *She has no accounting for taste in men!*

There's a sucker born every minute

P.T. Barnum, a famous American circus owner, once said that there was a sucker born every minute, in reference to some of the weird but fake circus attractions that people came to see. The expression quickly became a common reference to people who believe everything they hear.

a. *Diet pills sell well because there is a sucker born every minute.*
b. *Advertising is often based on the idea that there's a sucker born every minute.*
c. *If you listen to politicians it is easy to believe that a sucker is born every minute.*

Throw a curve

This is another expression from baseball, in which one of the key factors in the game is the ability of pitchers to throw curve balls. The expression is now used in a general sense of misleading or deceiving someone by some action or some comment.

a. *The distributor threw us a curve when he said that they wouldn't need any of our products until next year.*
b. *The CEO's announcement threw a curve into marketing program.*
c. *Just be sure you don't throw me a curve.*

Throw money at something

In recent times it has become common for people, companies and organizations in general to attempt to solve problems by the use of exceptional amounts of money—often in a reckless manner that does not have the effect desired. This practice is "throwing money" at the problem, with the inference being that the practice is short-sighted and may fail.

a. *When a problem comes up the first thing that many people think of is to throw money at it.*
b. *Throwing money at a problem without addressing the underlying causes is a foolish thing to do.*
c. *Many politicians become notorious for throwing money at problems.*

Throw someone to the wolves

Being "thrown to the wolves" suggests being eaten alive, so this expression has a powerful image. It means to deliberately expose someone to some kind of danger by revealing some secret about them, by firing them from a job, by putting them into some situation where they are unprotected and vulnerable to some kind of harm or serious disadvantage.

a. *I knew I had to be very careful to avoid being thrown to the wolves.*
b. *When the scientist made a false claim the university threw him to the wolves.*

c. *You'd better stay on his good side or he will throw you to the wolves.*

Throw up one's hands

"Throwing up one's hands" has traditionally been a sign of surrender, of giving up. The meaning has remained the same, but the expression is now used in a variety of other situations.

a. *When I heard that the negotiations had failed I throw my hands up in frustration.*
b. *Don't throw your hands up yet! We're not licked by a long shot!*
c. *You expect me to throw my hands up because of that little setback?*

Thumb one's nose

This reference to the nose refers to an attitude or an action that indicates disapproval, disfavor or refusal to obey. Originally it was expressed by some kind of hand signal that involved touching the nose.

a. *The boy thumbed his nose at me when I asked him to stop talking so loud.*
b. *It is rude to thumb your nose at anyone.*
c. *I wish you wouldn't thumb your nose at every suggestion I make.*

Tickled pink

When people laugh long and loud it may result in their faces becoming flushed a pinkish color, thus the expression "tickled pink". It means to be delighted, pleased, thrilled.

a. *I was tickled pink when I heard that she had agreed to go out with me.*
b. *When I heard she was coming I was tickled pink.*
c. *The whole audience was tickled pink at the funny comments made by the speaker.*

Tight ship

A "tight ship" refers to a ship whose captain and officers are very strict and manage the ship and its activities very diligently.

a. *My school teacher really ran a tight ship.*
b. *We're going to have to run a tight ship if we want to succeed.*
c. *You can tell that the company runs a tight ship just by watching the employees.*

Tight spot

A "tight spot" refers to a difficult situation, and is an extension of the idea that when one is tied up tight it is difficult or impossible to move.

a. *A sudden breakdown of the supply chain put us in a tight spot.*
b. *You are always getting yourself in a tight spot because you act without thinking!*
c. *Don't come crying to me the next time you get in a tight spot.*

Tighten one's belt

You may still have to tighten your belt if you lose weight, but this expression is now mostly used in reference to having less money to spend and having to cut down on your expenditures.

a. *When the price of gas goes up many people have to tighten their belt.*
b. *If we want to get through the month we'd better tighten our belt.*
c. *When I asked for a raise my boss told me to tighten my belt!*

Time is running out

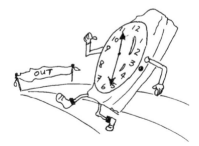

When there is a limit on the amount of time one has to accomplish something, and the time is about up, this expression acts as a warning to get ready, to speed things up.

a. *We have exactly one hour to finish this project, and time is running out.*
b. *Time is running out for women in their forties who want children.*
c. *I gave you an ultimatum, and time is running out.*

Tit for tat

Get back at someone; get revenge; usually in situations that are relatively minor, such as when kids or couples argue and each one tries to get in the last word.

a. *As long as you two keep up that tit for tat stuff you are not going to get anything resolved!*
b. *We went at it tit for tat for the rest of the day.*
c. *Don't get caught up in tit for tat behavior. It never works.*

Tits on a boar

Tits is a slang term for female breasts and a boar is a male pig, resulting in this expression being used to refer to something that is totally useless.

a. *Some people say that learning math is about as useful as tits on a boar!*
b. *He's about as useful as tits on a boar.*
c. *Most television programs are about as useful as tits on a boar.*

To the letter

When something is written into an agreement or contract the provisions are normally clear and concise, with the expectation that they will be "followed to the letter," meaning that will be followed exactly.

a. *I followed the contract to the letter, so why are you complaining?*
b. *The union negotiator followed the contract agreement to the letter.*
c. *That company does everything to the letter.*

Tongue-in-cheek

This is a euphemism for saying something that is meant to be ironic or facetious. Some people use the phrase in a purely joking manner.

a. *His speech was one tongue-in-cheek comment after the other.*
b. *Forget it! It was his tongue-in-cheek way of trying to be funny!*
c. *Some tongue-in-cheek comments are not funny!*

Turn a deaf ear

"Turning a deaf ear" to someone refers to pretending you didn't hear what was said, generally to avoid getting involved in something and avoid being obligated in any way.

a. *After a while I turned a deaf ear to all of the complaints being made about the new project.*
b. *I could tell the instant he turned a deaf ear to what I was saying.*
c. *Every time she turned a deaf ear to me she got a blank look on her face.*

Turn one's back on

The meaning of "turn your back" on someone who asks for or needs your help is easy to understand. It means refusing to help them.

a. *I was surprised and disappointed when he turned his back on me.*
b. *She said that if I turned my back on her she would never speak to me again.*
c. *I didn't turn my back on you! I didn't know you needed help!*

Turn one's stomach

Eating something that causes you to vomit is the source of this expression. It refers to anything that makes you feel sick or disgusted, from food and someone's behavior to the sight of something.

a. *The sight of the rotten meat turned my stomach.*
b. *His use of profanity turned my stomach.*
c. *The thought of spending all day with that group of idiots turns my stomach.*

Turn over a new leaf

Change one's life style or approach to things; generally said as a result of a desire to lose weight, get into better shape, look for a more satisfying job, stay out of trouble, and so on.

a. *When she confronted her husband about his drinking, he swore he would turn over a new leaf.*
b. *I wonder if he has turned over a new leaf.*
c. *I am always promising myself that I will turn over a new leaf.*

Turn the other cheek

This expression is from an old biblical saying that when someone strikes you on the cheek, turn the other cheek to your attacker instead of striking back.

a. *Turning the other cheek is not always the best thing to do.*
b. *When the bully hit me I wasn't about to turn the other cheek.*
c. *The service people were taught to turn the other cheek when they were berated by an angry customer.*

Turn the screws

A reference to tightening screws by turning them, and in earlier times a method of torture, this phrase is now mostly used in the sense of bringing pressure on someone to get them to do something.

a. *Turning the screws on him won't help! He's too tough!*
b. *Their way of negotiating is to turn the screws on you.*
c. *When I tried to back out she turned the screws on me.*

Turn the tables

This expression refers to suddenly changing the conditions of a situation to the point that it seriously disadvantages a person or a group of people.

a. *Before I realized what was going on she turned the tables on me.*
b. *Smart managers can often turn the tables on their competitors.*
c. *The students turned the tables on their teachers.*

Turn up one's nose

If you "turn your nose up" at something or somebody it means you do not think they are good enough, that they are worthy of you, or that they deserve any consideration.

a *My sister turned up her nose at a chance to teach in a nursing school.*
b. *Anybody who turns his or her nose up at an Infiniti automobile must have awfully high standards.*
c. *He never turns his nose up at any food as long as it is free.*

Turn up the heat

This saying means to literally turn up the heat in a place. It is also used to mean increasing the pressure on someone or some group to get them to do something.

a. *This room is cold. Let's turn up the heat.*
b. *When elections draw near politicians can be counted on to turn up the heat.*
c. *She turned the heat up on me so I had to agree with her.*

Twiddle one's thumbs

Just as it suggests, "twiddle one's thumbs" means to do nothing, to be idle.

a. *She twiddled her thumbs all year now she can't pass the final exams.*
b. *If you just sit around twiddling your thumbs you will never get done!*
c. *Stop twiddling your thumbs and get to work!*

Twist one's arm

"Twisting one's arm" used to be a method of physically torturing someone to force them to do something. Now it is used in a figurative sense to get people to do something you want them to do. Instead of actually twisting someone's arm you use persuasion, cajoling, begging, or make some kind of promise.

a. *I didn't want to go but my girlfriend kept twisting my arm.*
b. *I had to twist my friend's arm to get him to let me borrow his car.*
c. *I finally gave in to his arm-twisting and loaned him some money.*

Two heads are better than one

Two people acting together are often able to make better decisions than one person.

a. *I'd like to have your input on this thing. Two heads are better than one.*
b. *It is not always true that two heads are better than one.*
c. *If two heads are better than one are three heads better than two?*

Under a dark cloud

A dark cloud obscures the sunlight, making things look gloomy. People who are feeling down may be described as being under a dark cloud.

a. *She's been under a dark cloud ever since they broke up.*
b. *The boss is surely under a dark cloud today.*
c. *Why is everybody under a dark cloud?*

Under one's nose

Something that is right "under your nose" is something or some action that is very close to you, in sight and should be easily seen.

a. *It's right under your nose! Keep looking!*
b. *He carried on an affair right under her nose but she never caught on.*
c. *Sometimes it's the things that are under your nose that you can't see.*

Under the wire

"Under the wire" originally referred to wires that marked the boundary of something or the end of a line. It now refers to something occurring at the last moment.

a. *The money transfer was due at noon and we got it in just under the wire.*
b. *If we rush we can get this done just under the wire.*
c. *We made it under the wire with a few seconds to spare.*

Until hell freezes over

Hell is never going to freeze since by definition it is too hot, so this refers to something that is not going to happen.

a. *That will happen when hell freezes over!*
b. *Those two will never agree until hell freezes over!*
c. *Tell them I said I would accept their offer when hell freezes over!*

Up a tree

When a person doesn't know the answer, or has no idea what to do about a situation, he or she may be said to be up a tree, where the options are definitely limited. This phrase can be traced to the practice of climbing trees to escape predators or some other danger, and then being stuck there.

a. *If you do that, you are going to be up a tree for sure!*
b. *When it comes to things like that he is always up a tree!*
c. *I got myself up a tree by making a promise I couldn't keep.*

Up in arms

This expression is another old military term that refers to people taking up arms to defend themselves or attack someone. It is now used in reference to people getting angry at some situation and begin taking some kind of action, such as public demonstrations, speaking out, writing letters, to prevent some kind of action from occurring or to advance their own.

a. *Moments after the administration ordered the campus closed during lunch hour the students were up in arms.*
b. *If we don't give the employees a raise this year they will be up in arms in no time.*
c. *We don't want to get anybody up in arms so let's play it cool.*

Up one's sleeve

This saying probably came from the game of cards when cheaters would hide a card in one of their sleeves and put it in their hand or on the table when it was most advantageous to do so. It is used in reference to having something concealed for later use.

a. *The negotiator was famous for always having something up his sleeve.*
b. *If you've got anything up your sleeve now is the time to bring it out!*
c. *I promise you! I have nothing up my sleeve!*

Up the river without a paddle

If you are in a canoe or small boat without a paddle, you could be in trouble. This expression refers to a bad situation where there is no way out; no solution.

a. *If you sign that contract you will be up the river without a paddle!*
b. *He made a rash promise that put him up the river without a paddle.*
c. *That guy always seems to be up the river without a paddle.*

Up to my ass in alligators

When a person is especially busy trying to deal with so many different things he has no time to do anything else, he may say that he is up to his ass in alligators, meaning that he is consumed in trying to keep from being "eaten" alive by the situation.

a. *Ever since I took on this job I've been up to my ass in alligators!*
b. *He's always complaining that he is up to his ass in alligators.*
c. *He doesn't know what it means to really be up to his ass in alligators.*

Up to my ears/chin

This expression refers to having so much work or so many things to do that you cannot accept or do any more. The image is that of work or other obligations having piled up to the point that they reach your chin or your ears.

a. *When the new project was laid on my desk I was already up to my ears with work.*
b. *I don't know when I will finish this. I'm already up to my ears.*
c. *Come on! Give me a break! I'm already up to my chin.*

Upset the applecart

Naturally upsetting an applecart is disturbing—at least to the owner. This led to the expression "upset the applecart" being used in reference to actions that ruin a plan, whether done on purpose or by accident.

a. *Just when we were ready to sign a contract they introduced a new demand that upset the applecart.*
b. *He is so sensitive that it doesn't take much to upset his applecart.*
c. *He deliberately upset their applecart to get revenge for them snubbing him at a party.*

Warm up to someone

Begin to like someone, usually as a result of getting to know the person better over a period of time or because of something they do.

a. *She really turned me off at the beginning, but I gradually warmed up to her.*
b. *During our second meeting we gradually warmed up to each other.*
c. *He is really difficult to warm up to.*

Wash one's hands of

"Wash one's hands" has been extended to mean withdrawing from or refusing to be responsible for something, so it is no longer on or in your hands.

a. *I decided to wash my hands of the problem and let the secretary deal with it.*
b. *You can't just wash your hands of this problem and walk away!*
c. *My advice to you is wash your hands of the whole situation. It will only drag you down.*

Washed up

Washed up literally means cleaned up, but it is also used to mean that something or somebody is no longer capable, effective, or useful.

a. *Most athletes are washed up by the time they are 40.*
b. *What do you mean he's washed up as a politician?*
c. *My mother refused to believe she was washed up, even when she was 90 years old*

Water down

Mixing water with some other liquid to make it thinner or weaker is known as "watering it down." The term is now also used in the sense of making contracts, commitments and comments in general weaker.

a. *No sooner was the contract signed than he began trying to water it down.*
b. *She watered down her criticism when she saw how upset I was.*
c. *If we water down our demands our proposal may be accepted.*

We/they clicked

In this sense to "click with someone" means that you find out that you are compatible, that you have many things in common and feel good about each other. "Click" refers to the sound often made by metallic parts when they are joined together and fit perfectly.

a. *We clicked the moment we met, and have been together ever since.*

b. *I've never seen two people click so quickly.*
c. *It was obvious that the manager knew how to click with his employees.*

Wear the pants in the family

In earlier times men wore pants and women wore dresses. This gave rise to the expression "wear the pants in the family" as a comment on women who were more aggressive and bossy than their husbands.

a. *Nowadays it seems that many women wear the pants in their families.*
b. *Some men whose wives wear the pants in the family don't mind it at all.*
c. *Be careful! If you marry her she will wear the pants in your family!*

Welcome to the big leagues

"Big leagues" was originally from the world of sports, but it is now also used in business and other professions to mean the highest level and the most demanding, as when someone joins a world-class enterprise, such as IBM.

a. *Well, I see you've made it to the big leagues.*
b. *This is my last chance to make it to the big leagues!*
c. *When I became vice president my friends sent me a message saying, "Welcome to the big leagues!"*

Welcome to the real world

Some people, like students, never face really serious challenges in their daily lives, and often have a distorted view of what it is like for others. They may encounter this expression when they find themselves facing problems other people face.

a. *At the graduation ceremony, the commencement speaker ended his speech by saying, "Welcome to the real world!"*
b. *You have to learn how to face the real world; not the world of your imagination.*
c. *He just never grew up; never faced the real world.*

Wet behind the ears

Someone who is immature, childish, inexperienced is described as wet behind the ears, from the fact that children just learning how to wash and dry their faces often do not dry behind their ears.

a. *He comes on as a grown man but is actually still wet behind the ears.*
b. *I was embarrassed when she told me I was still wet behind the ears.*
c. *Stop acting like you are wet behind the ears!*

Wet your whistle

Taking an alcoholic drink is sometimes referred to as wetting you whistle. The saying may derive from the fact that wetting your lips makes it easier to whistle.

a. *Man! I'm hot and tired. Let's go wet our whistle!*
b. *The first thing I'm going to do when I get home is wet my whistle!*
c. *If you wet your whistle too often you may get into trouble.*

What goes around comes around

Life has a way of evening all things out. If you mistreat someone chances are you will pay for it some way in the future. If you tell a lie it will make come back to haunt you.

a. *You're setting yourself up for a fall! Remember, what goes around comes around!*
b. *He lied about her but got the worst of it because what goes around comes around.*
c. *He cheated on the exam but didn't get the job because what goes around comes around.*

When push comes to shove

This expression refers to reaching a stalemate, when some drastic action is required to make progress.

a. *When push comes to shove, he always manages to come up with some*

creative solution.
b. *We need a new marketing program before push comes to shove.*
c. *Their team is especially good when push comes to shove.*

When the crunch comes

Crunch was originally used in reference to the crackling, grinding sound made when chewing something hard. Now it also refers to a situation in which demand exceeds supply, causing a shortage, when something is at a make or break point, as in a ball game, or when negotiations are at a critical point.

a. *When the crunch came, the company finally began making plans to open a new factory.*
b. *When the crunch came all we could do was work harder.*
c. *With the score tied, I knew it was crunch time.*

White elephant

The expression "white elephant" apparently grew out of the fact that purely white elephants are exceedingly rare (if there ever has been one), and are therefore associated with things that are not popular, not useful, pointless, and unnecessary.

a. *As soon as the new airport construction was announced it was criticized as a white elephant.*
b. *The new factory turned out to be a white elephant.*
c. *Somebody recently said that the new government was no better than a herd of white elephants.*

White lie

The color white has long been associated with things that are good and desirable, thus a "white lie" is seen as harmless, as told just to be polite, to make someone feel good rather than bad.

a. *I told my boss a white lie just to keep things harmonious.*
b. *When it comes to telling white lies she is a master!*
c. *You may consider that a white lie but I don't!*

Wild-eyed and bushy tailed

When cornered and in danger, some animals get wild-eyed and raise their tails up in a threatening move. It now refers to being very aggressive, very active, and very enthusiastic, usually in a positive sense.

a. *I've never seen anyone that wild-eyed and bushy tailed!*
b. *He is looking for young people who are wild-eyed and bushy tailed!*
c. *The new crop of employees came on as wild-eyed and bushy tailed.*

Wind up

One of the original meanings of "wind" is to encircle something or wrap it up. "Wind up" is an expansion of the term, and means to come to the end; to finish.

a. *The meeting will wind up at 4 p.m.*
b. *We need to wind this up no latter than this evening to make our deadline.*
c. *The game was scheduled to wind up in an hour but went into overtime.*

Wing it

"Wing" in this expression refers to the wings of a bird, and gives an image of something moving or flying. "Wing it" means to do something or move forward on something without any specific method or plan, just doing whatever seems appropriate or right at the time.

a. *He has no plan. He's just winging it.*
b. *Look! We cannot just wing this project! We have to have a plan!*
c. *Okay! If that's the way you feel about it, we'll wing it.*

Wink at

"Wink at" refers to rapidly and deliberately closing an eyelid, and is widely used in the United States as a means of flirting with the opposite sex, and conveying a conspiratorial message. "Wink at" also refers to closing one's eyes, or ignoring, something that is against the rules or against the law.

a. *Stop winking at that girl!*
b. *Well, she winked at me first!*
c. *I don't mind winking at breaking small rules, but not big ones.*

Wipe that smile off your face!

Be serious; stop joking. This can be a casual, humorous expression or one that is deadly serious.

a. *If you don't wipe that smile off your face I'll do it for you!*
b. *This is serious! You'd better wipe that smile off your face!*
c. *It took me several minutes to wipe the smile off my face.*

With flying colors

Posting banners, flags and pennants on high poles has long been a way of celebrating or marking events, resulting in the expression "with flying colors," which refers to something that was done successfully.

a. *She passed the course with flying colors and wants to go out and celebrate.*
b. *The new product passed the most rigorous tests with flying colors.*
c. *If this technology does not pass with flying colors we're in trouble.*

With open arms

The phrase "with open arms" already has a positive image, and when used as an expression its implications are even more positive. It refers to accepting or greeting someone eagerly, warmly and with enthusiasm.

a. *The prime minister was welcomed with open arms when he came to visit our city.*
b. *We welcomed the newcomers with open arms.*
c. *The newcomers were overjoyed when we welcomed them with open arms.*

Wolf in sheep's clothing

This saying refers to a person (usually a man) who acts very nice, polite and innocent, but actually is just the opposite and makes a practice of taking advantage of women and others. Most often said of men who take advantage of naïve women for sexual purposes.

a. *Don't go out with him! He's a wolf in sheep's clothing!*
b. *Her new boyfriend turned out to be a wolf in sheep's clothing.*
c. *Sometimes I wish I could be a wolf in sheep's clothing!*

Word of honor

Giving one's "word of honor" is the equivalent of a sworn, solemn oath that what one said is true or that he or she will not fail to keep an obligation.

a. *It's the truth! My word of honor!*
b. *He gave his word of honor and then broke it.*
c. *I won't need a contract if you give me your word of honor.*

Work out

"Work out" now has two basic uses. It is commonly used in reference to taking physical exercise, in a gymnasium, on a sports field or in some kind of fitness club. It is also used in the sense of planning something, of coming up with solutions to problems.

a. *Many people now work out as a regular part of their lifestyle.*
b. *We have to get this problem worked out soon.*
c. *Let's work out a budget for the new project.*

Worth its weight in gold

Something that is very valuable. It can be an idea or something that is physical, like a process or a product.

a. *Sony's original transistor radio turned out to be worth its weight in gold.*
b. *It will be worth its weight in gold if we can get a patent.*
c. *He turned out to be worth his weight in gold.*

Wrap things up

When something is wrapped up, the implication is that it is ready to go. This phrase is also used to mean to end some action, such as work or play.

a. *Let's wrap this up and go home.*
b. *You could tell he was trying to wrap up his overlong presentation.*
c. *I wrapped things up with a joke.*

Write off

This colloquial expression refers to removing or eliminating something from a business record; such as canceling a debt or loss. You simple delete it from your records. It may also be used in reference to relationships and other things.

a. *No matter what you say I am not going to write off that loan!*
b. *Rich countries sometimes write off debts owed to them by poor countries.*
c. *I told her I was never going to see her again; that I was going to write her off!*

You can't fight city hall

"City Hall" has traditionally been used in the United States to mean the local town or city government. The figurative meaning of this saying is that you can't win in a dispute with the local government.

a. *You may as well stop trying to get a building permit. You can't fight city hall!*
b. *He spent all of his money fighting city hall.*
c. *I don't believe you can't fight city hall. You just have to fight harder.*

Your own worst enemy

Some people say things and do things that cause them more trouble than their worst enemies.

a. *You talk too much! You are your own worst enemy!*
b. *He was always his own worst enemy.*
c. *That teacher's bad mood makes him his own worst enemy.*

Zero in on

To focus on something. (This expression reminds me of the Japanese combat planes used during World War II that were known to Americans as "Zeros." During the early years of the war, they were superior to American fighter planes, making "zero in on" a common expression.)

a. *If we are going to make this product a success we have to zero in on the right market.*
b. *If you don't zero in on something and stick to it you will never succeed.*
c. *The secret to his success was his ability to zero in on problems.*